400 YEARS

ACROSS THE OCEAN

"THE BIRTH OF AMERICA"

400 YEAR ANNIVERSARY

PILGRIM LANDING
IN AMERICA
1620

MAYFLOWER

PILGRIM PLANTATION

TO A NEW WORLD
ALSO
AMERICA'S GREATEST MYSTERY

The seven lost survivors &
secret of Roanoke Island

WALTER SAWYER

CITI OF
BOOKS

CITIOFBOOKS, INC.
3736 Eubank NE Suite A1
Albuquerque, NM 87111-3579
www. citiofbooks. com

Hotline: 1 (877) 389-2759
Fax: 1 (505) 930-7244

Ordering Information:
Quantity sales. Special discounts are available on quantity purchases by corporations, associations, and others. For details, contact the publisher at the address above.

Printed in the United States of America.

| ISBN-13: | Softcover | 978-1-963209-62-4 |
| | eBook | 978-1-963209-63-1 |

Library of Congress Control Number: 2024902840

400 YEARS
ACROSS THE OCEAN

"THE BIRTH OF AMERICA"

400 YEAR ANNIVERSARY

PILGRIM LANDING
IN AMERICA
1620

MAYFLOWER

PILGRIM PLANTATION

TO A NEW WORLD
ALSO
AMERICA'S GREATEST MYSTERY

The seven lost survivors &
secret of Roanoke Island

WALTER SAWYER

TABLE OF CONTENTS

Preface v

The Pilgrim Adventure Started in 1578 1

Pilgrims Arrive in America 4

Where Did the Pilgrims and Puritans Come From? 7

Motivations for the Voyage 9

Speedwell and Mayflower 13

The Mayflower Sets Sail 16

Arrival in America 20

Passengers 25

Mayflower Ship History 30

Later History 55

Legacy 57

The Story of Thanksgiving 60

Four Hundredth Anniversary, 2020 62

Girls on the Mayflower 63

The Lost Colony of Roanoke 67

Jamestown 70

Glossary of Ships 76

Jamestown 84

Conclusion 87

Bibliography 88

References 90

Further Reading 95

About the Author 97

Be a Pilgrim for
"One Day"
Have Some Fun, Dress as a Pilgrim on Thanksgiving Day
November 24th, 2022
Only Two Requirements:
Dress as a Pilgrim and bring the
Family as Pilgrims, also.
Name of ship and cruise line to be announced
Point of contact:
Walter Sawyer
772.336.8624

I have played the part of John Alden, carpenter, on three occasions aboard the Princess Cruise Line over the course five years.

Make memories you will enjoy for years to come.

In the autumn of 1620, while anchored in Cape Cod Bay, the Pilgrims' small ship became the birthplace of our nation's constitutional tradition. Historian Henry Culver called the Mayflower "the wave-rocked cradle of our liberties." The Plymouth colonists and Native peoples of the region, mariners and traders who met along New England's shores of change, created a new society—sometimes in conflict, sometimes in collaboration. They crafted a region rich in intellect, spirituality, self-government, and commerce—a place of creative splendors whose influence on American culture and the world is inestimable.

Preface

I would like to thank the many sources who supply the information for this book. In researching, I tried to keep the information as accurate as possible.

I would like to thank Ann Mallardi for giving me the idea when we took our first Thanksgiving cruise. Since then, we have taken two other Thanksgiving cruisers, always playing the part of Pricilla Mullen and John Alden.

My biggest reason for writing this book was my heritage; it is something to be proud of and the need for children to know their heritage.

Since childhood, I remember my grandparents talking about their ancestors coming from the old country, on the Mayflower. We would ask questions about who are we were related to; their response was "John Alden."

I remember going to Plymouth Rock on a school field trip, with my classmates. I remember going to the cranberry factory, about a half mile from the rock where they made cranberry sauce. In Plymouth square, where they made manila rope for ships, on the second floor of the factory, history is everywhere; all you have to do is look and enjoy the surroundings. As I remember, several restaurants serve seafood of all types.

We visited Plymouth Plantation where the Pilgrims set up housekeeping in 1620. We walked through one house, then another to see how they lived. All the cooking was done in a stone fireplace with hanging cooking pots. Fireplaces keep the house warm in the winter and summer.

Their hardships showed in the ten-by-ten room with a loft, where the children slept. Attached to the house where the garden and the animal are corralled nearby, I enjoyed returning to Plymouth three or four times over the last fifty years.

I thought it would be encouraging to bring the story of America history into the school system. Our children are our future.

Unfortunately, school education is melting away; it takes the community to do their share.

Children in school do not know our countries history; something has to be done to educate them. Rita (a member in the American Legion) knew teachers in the local school system. This opened the door into two schools and three fifth grade class.

They took the opportunity and asked for a community speaker, in our case, to talk about the Pilgrims to their students. Several years later, I contacted my local elementary school system again. Sadly, they never contacted me to address the children again.

The reason why I wrote this book.

I wanted to take a Thanksgiving cruise and enjoy some real excitement by dressing up as Pilgrims, with my Ann. I also knew the importance of this piece of history has to be shared.

We took advantage of my exploits and went dancing at a local hotel on Hutchinson Island on Friday night. On this particular occasion, it was Halloween, and we chose to attend. There were about thirty couples dressed in various costumes. We came in second place.

The following day, being Saturday was another dance at the civic center, we dressed up in Pilgrim attire. We won first prize.

Bring Pilgrims into the community.

Halloween time was our first outside activity at Botanical Garden.

Dressed in Pilgrim attire, a group of community organizations got together and passed out candy to the children, who were dressed up in Halloween costumes.

We stood in an assigned area, talked with parents and children as they walked by. Ann and I were dressed in Pilgrim attire. We portrayed Pricilla Mullen and John Alden. We stayed until dark, talking with the adults and children in their Halloween costumes.

Every year, for six years, we were asked to share our story with the kids. We found many families who home schooled their children and were now able to educate them.

I met one mother who home schooled her children. Along the way, they would answer questions about Pilgrims and how we started a new nation, America. I also met a student who knew very little and another who didn't know anything at all. Many stood and asked what the banner was for the four hundredth anniversary of Pilgrims landing in America.

Pricilla would be his future wife, bearing ten children according to history. We talked about the *Mayflower*, people's living conditions aboard the ship, how they lived over sixty-six days on the high seas. During stormy weather, hot food was available every third day.

Passengers lived in damp conditions from seawater coming down the hatch. Our talk lasted for over twenty-five minutes.

While in church, years later, I asked the principal from a local school to fix it up so I could address children. I would talk about the Pilgrims who came over on the *Mayflower*. No luck with a response.

Our First Cruise

We went on the Coral Princess, to the Caribbean, for our cruise. We intentionally chose this cruise because of it being a Thanksgiving adventure. Ann and I dressed as Pilgrims: Pricilla Mullen and John Alden I got cold feet walking out the cabin door, dressed in Pilgrim attire.

Ann, dressed as Pricilla Mullen, said, "You got me this far, we are going all the way." Walking out the cabin door, the hallway was empty. From nowhere, a man came up to us and said, "Now this really feels like a real Thanksgiving." Passengers stared at us as we walked toward the elevator.

It was an adventure walking into a crowd dressed up in Pilgrims' oached the dining room entrance, they pushed us to the head of the line, thinking we were part of the ship's crew staff, probably.

Walking through the crowed tables and wishing them a Happy Thanksgiving, many asked us if they could take pictures with us. We consented, telling them we were passengers also, just having a good experience, as well as a good time, on our cruise. There were so many passengers asking why were dressed in this attire. One out of three guests on the ship were from different countries.

Going down the elevator to the fifth deck, we walked into another crowd, in line for dinner. They, too, rushed us forward and asked for pictures. We must have had our picture taken thirty or more times, once they found we were passengers also.

The head chef walked up to us and asked what we thought of the Thanksgiving meal. Truthfully, being from New England and enjoying a real Thanksgiving dinner, I proceeded to tell him what our meals were like; they were different than we ever had here. It must have worked as the next meal on the menu was, as I described the night before, turkey and gravy, cranberry sauce, mashed potato, hot rolls, squash, and apple pie.

I wrote to the cruise line, telling than of our experience. I also shared the comments from the passengers who lived in other counties.

Several years later, we took another cruise, with the same cruise line, looking forward to enjoying the same adventure.

Follow-Up: Second Cruise

Then three years later, we targeted this holiday because it was Thanksgiving. We wanted to dress up and have some fun, again. On our latest cruise, aboard the Emerald Princess, our trip was to the Panama Cannel, Thanksgiving Day, November 25, 2021. We dressed as John Alden, carpenter and his wife, Pricilla Mullen.

We dressed in Pilgrims' attire to attend the Thanksgiving 8 a.m. church service. We called it a day when we took our clothes off by 9 p.m.

We had our picture taken at lease eighty times and had shipmates make the comment, "This is truly Thanksgiving Day." Smiles were the action of the day, along with thumbs-up signs.

Many have wished they had thought of dressing up as a Pilgrim. I even found the relatives of William Bradford, the first governor of Massachusetts. John Alden and Gov. William Bradford signed the Mayflower Compact; they laid the ground work for the first Massachusetts state Constitution.

The one thing I cannot get over is the number of folks who have no knowledge of our Thanksgiving holiday. They are from other counties; they, too, wanted to take pictures and several joined in the pictures. I never knew that Canada also has a Thanksgiving in October.

The Indian on the Massachusetts shield was Chief Massasoit (1580–1661), as he was known to the Mayflower Pilgrims. He was the leader of the Wampanoag tribe, also known as the Grand Sachem as well as Ousemequin (sometimes spelled Woosamequen). Massasoit played a major role in the success of the Pilgrims.

Conventional narratives of Massasoit paint the picture of a friendly Indigenous person who came to the aid of the starving Pilgrims.

The official state motto of Massachusetts is *"Ense petit placidam sub libertate quietem"* (English translation: "By the sword we seek peace, but peace only under liberty").

Chief Massasoit (1580–1661), as he was known to the Mayflower Pilgrims, was the leader of the Wampanoag tribe.

Published by the History Science News, January 8, 2019.

Samoset, one of the first Native Americans to meet the Pilgrims, famously introduced them to Squanto.

The Pilgrim Adventure Started in 1578

Squanto Captured about 1605

Squanto was one of many tribe members watching an English ship sailing into Plymouth Harbor, America, when sailors' landed, about 1605.

The tribe sent several canoes to meet the ship on their arrival. The captain of the ship assured them, "We come in peace." Mingling with the tribe, the cohorts Squanto and Epenusa (a tribe member) helped them with the trade goods, going into the hull of the ship.

Squanto was recently married. Nakoona stood on the shore and watched Squanto and Epenusa board the ship and sail away.

For sixty-six days, both Indians were prisoners in the hull of the ship. Anxious to find out where they were going and how long they would be in captivity, they were frustrated.

In the hold, Squanto wanted their hands free so they could eat. He still took the advantage to learn as much as he could about his captives. He learned the Plymouth Shipping Co. belonged to Sir George of England.

When the ship arrived, he was transported by carriage to the center of the city and into a big building, where hundreds of the city folks were seated.

The noble salvages were placed on display for all England to see in a circus arena. A brown bear came out with the intent

1

of killing Squanto. After a couple of misses, Squanto started singing an Indian melody. Almost at once, the bear lay down and the audience became quiet.

TaSir, advanced of the situation, escaped out of the ring and on top of roofs, jumped from several house along their ridges. He landed in green fields, running as fast as he could go, into the countryside.

Squanto found a canoe; he had one thing in mind: get as far as he could. The canoe tipped over in the high seas, later washed up on a deserted beach, where a monk found him. Brother Daniel did all he could to the almost-dead Indian.

Squanto learned a great deal from Brother Daniel and the other monks. Brother Daniel took him to a monastery where he learned about horses and religion. The greatest gift was patience: the ability to endure waiting, delay, or provocation without becoming annoyed or upset or to persevere calmly when faced with difficulties.

Brother Daniel gained his confidence and was allowed to leave the compound through an open gate.

He was showed how to ride a horse; in exchange he showed the monks how to make moccasins. He also showed the monks how to make popcorn out of whole ears of corn.

Squanto had a chance to see the Pilgrims William Bradford and Samuel Fuller soliciting a ship to leave England for the New World. Sir George made a statement: "I cannot see why anyone would want to leave England."

Squanto heard loud noises in the monastery library. He stood and watched Sir George Henmen looked through around a two-inch, handcrafted designed Bible. Father Monk made a pledge, "No salvation was here."

Squanto questioned why they didn't retaliate for the action. Brother Daniel said, "It does not benefit anyone."

Squanto, in leaving the monastery, left the feather given to him by his wife, Nakoona, on their wedding day, as a token of friendship.

Epenusa returned to the seaport town and boarded with "demijohn" tied up. He noticed the amount of rats running around and coated his leather straps with his food laid alongside him. He just laid on the hay, with hands propped on his chest. He waited for the rats to have a meal on the straps, which would free him.

Squanto could not forget what Sir George said: "The picking order: God, angels, sir, the people, and you are the lowest on the chain." Epenusa promised Sir George there was gold in his village.

Squanto broke free and ran through the streets for the awaiting ship. He grabbed a horse Brother Daniel brought for him. Squanto rode for the ship that was passing by the pier and jumped to the ship. He landed on the deck.

To his surprise, the Indian who was captive with him was laying on deck. Sir George wanted to do business with him in America.

Squanto's Return to America

As the sixty-day trip ended his fifteen-year captivity, Squanto learned of his tribe's demise. He had to see for his self and disappeared into the woods.

Pilgrims Arrive in America

A boat of Pilgrims landed, and two members of the ship's company were killed. Squanto became the peacemaker and calmed the Indian and the Pilgrim down; both were on the edge of a full-scale war.

Squanto pointed out that killing each other would not resolve anything, except result in a lot of dead bodies. He pointed out, "We live under one moon, one Earth, and under one sky, so let's all live together." This peace was kept for over fifty years.

Squanto showed the Pilgrims his skills years and huts and helped the Pilgrims survive the New England winter then they built the new homes a short distance away.

Wampanoag Indian hut at Plymouth Plantation in Plymouth, Massachusetts

The Pilgrims started constructing their living houses and storehouses in late December 1620 but only managed to get a couple built before and during the first winter. They were hindered not only by the weather but by occasional fires usually caused by a spark or ember from the fire making it onto the roof. The roof was constructed of dried thatch.

The following diseases were brought to America by sailors when they landed on these foreign shores. These diseases were contracted by people who had no way of fighting off them. Consequently, these diseases wipe out many small and entire villages.

Smallpox

When Squanto walked through his village, the empty huts were falling apart because of time and the lack of upkeep. He told the story of his fate brought by other sailing ships. Smallpox is a mayoclinic-diseases.

Before the Pilgrims settled in the New World, an epidemic of smallpox had killed a large portion of the Pequot Indians. The first symptoms of smallpox usually appear ten to fourteen days after you're infected.) During the incubation period of seven to seventeen days, you look and feel healthy and can't infect others. Following the incubation period, a sudden onset of flu-like signs and symptoms occurs. These include fever, overall discomfort, headache, severe fatigue, severe back pain, and vomiting. Possibly a few days later, flat, red spots appear first on your face, hands, and forearms, and later on your trunk. The New England Native Americans had no abilities to fight off the contagious diseases.

Scurvy

The symptoms of scurvy tend to start out slowly and worsen over time. They tend to be vague, so you might not realize that you or your child is experiencing the effects of this nutritional deficit. Common symptoms of scurvy include: fatigue and muscle pain, loss of appetite, stiff and swollen joints, spontaneous bleeding and bruising, petechiae, gingivitis, and ulceration of your rash or blisters. Also known as scorbutic, it is a medical condition caused by a lack of vitamin C. Left untreated, scurvy can be fatal, but fortunately this condition is extremely easy to address, as all that is required to eliminate scurvy is an increase of vitamin C intake. Many settlers died within of scurvy and malnutrition during that horrible first winter. Of the 102 original Mayflower passengers, only forty-four survived.

Cholera

Cholera is an acute diarrhea disease caused by a toxin produced by various strains of a comma-shaped gram-negative bacterium of the genus Vibrio (V. cholera synonym V. comma) when it is present in large numbers in the proximal part of the human small intestine, it can be fatal.

The Mayflower at sea, drawing from a book, c. 1893 (Painter unknown)

Where Did the Pilgrims and Puritans Come From?

Their leadership came from the religious congregations of Brownists, or Separatist Puritans, who had fled religious persecution in England for the tolerance of seventeenth-century Holland.

Like many New England towns and villages, the name originated across the pond—from the original Plymouth, in Devon, England. That name is derived from the River Plym, which opens into a bay (or mouth). In 1616, Captain John Smith, of the Jamestown, Virginia, settlement—the nation's very first, was established in 1607. It was named after King James I. He been exploring the northeast coast of America when he came upon a river and bay in today's Plymouth. The geography reminded him of River Plym and the bay in England.

The *Mayflower* was an English ship that transported a group of English families known today as the Pilgrims from England to the New World in 1620. After a grueling ten weeks at sea, the *Mayflower*, with 102 passengers and a crew of about thirty, reached America. They dropped anchor near the tip of Cape Cod, Massachusetts, on November 21 (November 11), 1620. There were more than twenty-six ships named after the *Mayflower*.

Differing from their contemporaries, the Puritans (who sought to reform and purify the Church of England), the Pilgrims chose to separate themselves from the Church of England because they believed that it was beyond redemption due to its Roman Catholic past and the church's resistance to reform, which forced them to pray in private. Starting in 1608, a group of English families left England for Holland, where they could worship freely. By 1620, the community determined to cross the Atlantic for America, which they considered a "new promised land," where they would establish Plymouth Colony.

The painting was digitally refined to convey a scene of desolate beauty at the end of the Pilgrims' long journey to an unfamiliar New World. Art director Greg Breeding designed the stamp with original art by Greg Harlin.

Motivations for the Voyage

Plymouth History, Pilgrims Setting Up Their Colony

A congregation of approximately four hundred English Protestants living in exile in Leiden, Holland, were dissatisfied with the failure of the Church of England to reform what they felt were many excesses and abuses. But rather than work for change in England (as other Puritans did), they chose to live as Separatists in religiously tolerant Holland in 1608. As separatists, they were considered illegal radicals by their home country of England.

The government of Leiden was recognized for offering financial aid to reformed churches, whether English, French or German, which made it a sought-after destination for Protestant intellectuals. Many of the separatists were illegal members of a church in Nottinghamshire, England, secretly practicing their Puritan form of Protestantism. When they learned that the authorities were aware of their congregation, church members fled during the night with little more than the clothes they were wearing and clandestinely made it to Holland.

Van Swanenburg of workers in Leiden's wool industry (Painting by Isaac Claesz)

Life in Holland became increasingly difficult for the congregation. They were forced into menial and backbreaking jobs, such as cleaning wool, which led to a variety of health issues. In addition, several of the country's leading theologians began engaging in open debates which led to civil unrest. This instilled fear that Spain might again place Holland's population under siege, as it had done years earlier. England's James I subsequently formed an alliance with Holland against Spain, with a condition outlawing independent English church congregations in Holland. Thus formed the separatists' motivating factors to sail for the New World, with the benefit of being beyond the reach of King James and his bishops.

Their desire to travel to America was considered audacious and risky, as previous attempts to settle in North America had failed. Jamestown, founded in 1607, saw most four hundred of the five hundred new arrivals. Four hundred forty died of starvation during the first six months of winter. The Puritan separatists also learned of the constant threat of attacks by indigenous peoples. But despite all the arguments against traveling to this new land, their conviction that God wanted them to go held say: "We verily believe and trust the Lord is with us," they wrote, "and that He will graciously prosper our endeavors, according to the simplicity of our hearts therein."

Decision to Leave Holland

After deciding to leave Holland, they planned to cross the Atlantic using two purchased ships. A small ship with the name Speedwell would first carry them from Leiden to England, then the larger Mayflower would be used to transport most of the passengers and supplies the rest of the way.

Pilgrims: John Carver, William Bradford, and Miles Standish, at prayer during their voyage to North America. (Robert W. Weir,

https://en.wikipedia.org/wiki/File:Embarkation_of_the_Pilgrims.jpg1844 painting)

Not all of the separatists were able to depart as many did not have enough time to settle their affairs, and their budgets were too meager to buy the necessary travel supplies. The congregation, therefore, decided that the younger and stronger members should go first, with others possibly following in the future. Although the congregation had been led by John Robinson, who first proposed the idea of emigrating to America, he chose to remain in Leiden to care for those who could not make the voyage.

John Robinson explained to his congregation why they should emigrate, he used the analogy of the ancient Israelites leaving Babylon to escape bondage by returning to Jerusalem, where they would build their temple. "The Pilgrims and Puritans actually referred to them as God's New Israel," writes Peter Marshall. It was, therefore, the "Manifest Destiny" to the Pilgrims and Puritans to similarly build a "spiritual Jerusalem" in America.

When it was time to leave, the ship's senior leader, Edward Winslow, described the scene of families being separated at the departure: "A flood of tears poured out. Those not sailing accompanied us to the ship, but were not able to speak to one another for the abundance of sorrow before parting." William Bradford, another leader who would be the second governor of the Plymouth Colony, similarly described the departure:

Truly doleful was the sight of that sad and mournful parting To see what sighs and sobs and prayers did sound among them; what tears did gush from every eye, and pithy speeches pierced each heart...their Reverend Pastor, falling down on his knees, and the congregation followed.

The trip to the south coast of England took three days, where the ship took anchor at Southampton on August 5 (July 26), 1620. From there, the Pilgrims first laid eyes on their larger ship, the Mayflower, as it was being loaded with provisions.

Speedwell and Mayflower

Mayflower II, a replica of the original Mayflower docked at Plymouth, Massachusetts

Carrying about sixty-five passengers, the Mayflower left London in mid-July 1620. The ship then preceded down the Thames to the south coast of England, where it anchored at Southampton, Hampshire. There she waited for the planned rendezvous on July 22 with the Speedwell, coming from Holland with members of the Leiden congregation. Although both ships planned to depart for America by the end of July, a leak was discovered on the Speedwell, which had to be repaired.

Walking down the dock, seeing the Mayflower anchored in the harbor, I wonder who will be boarding her? There are woman, children, and husbands standing in line to board the long boat. A long boat lying against the dock will be taking us out to board her.

John Alden announces his qualification to Captain Jones as a carpenter, barrel maker, shipbuilder, and cooper.

Captain Jones informs John Alden that the passengers

are the ones who will be needing a carpenter when they reach their destination in the New World. The carpenter must agree to sign on for a one-year contract. I have had the same one for past voyages.

Climbing up the ship chain ladder (against the hull) hanging from the main deck, passengers each took their turn onto the main deck.

Carrying their belongings for the long trip, bags and baggage, they worked their way to the ladder that would lead them to the lower deck. Each person would have to back down the stairway, step by step. Into the darkness from the daylight, the white overhead brightened everything around them.

The living area, thirty feet wide from starboard to port (side to side) and fifty-five from bow to stern, would be their two-deck living area.

The Pilgrim passengers list had seventy-two, with a crew of thirty. The Pilgrims and crew would have their own food supply, while the water will be supply for all. The passengers' list will increases to 102 in an already tight quarters.

The Pilgrim are under the assumption that they will be traveling under the Virginia Company. The agreement is they will work for five days over seven years.

The ships set sail for America around August 5, but the *Speedwell* sprang another leak shortly after, which necessitated the ships' return to Dartmouth for repairs. They made a new start after the repairs, but more than 200 miles (320 km) beyond Land's End at the southwestern tip of England, the Speedwell sprang a third leak. It was now early September, and they had no choice but to abandon the

Speedwell and make a determination on her passengers. This was a dire event, as vital funds had been wasted on the ship, which were considered very important to the future success of their settlement in America. Both ships returned to Plymouth, where thirty *Speedwell* passengers joined the now-overcrowded *Mayflower* while the others returned to Holland.

They waited for seven more days until the wind picked up. William Bradford was especially worried: "We lie here waiting for as fair a wind as can blow… Our victuals will be half eaten up, I think, before we go from the coast of England; and, if our voyage last long, we shall not have a month's victuals when we come in the country." According to Bradford, the *Speedwell* was refitted and seaworthy, having "made many voyages…to the great profit of her owners." He suggested that the *Speedwell's* master may have used "cunning and deceit" to abort the voyage by causing the leaks, fearing starvation and death in America.

The Mayflower Sets Sail

At last, the over-full and hitherto baffled *Mayflower* was ready for the third trial. This final voyage would be successful. On September 26, 1620, there were gallant little craft slipped out to sea. In proportion to her cubic feet of space, no heavier cargo had ever been shipped across the Atlantic. The entirety of a new church, a new commonwealth, a new nation, all of which were to bless the world, were confined within the limits of the Mayflower's hold. The course of empire was moving westward indeed.

—Rev. E. W. Bishop

In 1608, early September, western gales turned the North Atlantic into a dangerous place to sail. The *Mayflower's* provisions were already quite low when departing Southampton, and they became lower still by delays of more than a month. The passengers had been onboard the ship this entire time, feeling worn out and in no condition for a very taxing, lengthy Atlantic journey cooped up in the cramped spaces of a small ship.

When the *Mayflower* sailed from Plymouth alone on September 16 (September 6), 1620, with what Bradford called "a prosperous wind," she carried 102 passengers plus a crew of twenty-five to thirty officers and men, bringing the total aboard to approximately 130. At about 180 tons, she was considered a smaller cargo ship, having traveled mainly between England and Bordeaux with clothing and wine, not an ocean ship. Nor was she in good shape, as she was sold for scrap four years after her Atlantic voyage. She was a high built craft forward and aft measuring approximately 100 feet (30 m) in length and about 25 feet (7.6 m) at her widest point.

With couples packed closely together for a trip lasting two months, a great deal of trust and confidence was required among everyone aboard.

John Carver, one of the leaders on the ship, often inspired the Pilgrims with a "sense of earthly grandeur and divine purpose." He was later called the "Moses of the Pilgrims," notes historian John Meacham. The Pilgrims "believed they had a covenant like the Jewish people of old," writes author Rebecca Frasier. "America was the new Promised Land." In a similar vein, early American writer James Russell Lowell stated, "Next to the fugitives whom Moses led out of Egypt, the little shipload of outcasts who landed at Plymouth are destined to influence the future of the world."

The first half of the voyage proceeded over calm seas and under pleasant skies. Then the weather changed, with continuous northeasterly storms hurling themselves against the ship, and huge waves constantly crashing against the topside deck. In the midst of one storm, the servant of physician Samuel Fuller died and was buried at sea. A baby was also born, christened Oceanus Hopkins. During another storm, so fierce were the winds that the sails could not be used; the ship was forced to drift without hoisting its sails for days, or else risk losing her masts. The storm washed a male passenger, John Howland, overboard.

He had sunk about twelve feet until a crew member threw out a rope, which Howland managed to grab, and he was safely pulled back on board.

Mayflower II cabin interior for 102 passengers

The passengers were forced to crouch in semi-darkness below deck as ocean swells rose to over a hundred feet. With waves tossing the boat in different directions, men held onto their wives, who themselves held onto their children. Water was soaking everyone and everything above and below deck.

Captain Jones ordered the sea anchor put out (sea anchor: its purpose is to stabilize the vessel and to limit progress through the water, It is a device that is streamed from a boat in heavy weather) to keep the ship under control. The seas hit the ship bow with great force; each wave was bigger than the last. The sails on the main mast canvas ripped the full length.

In mid-ocean, the ship came close to being totally disabled and may have had to return to England or risk sinking. A storm had so badly damaged its main beam that even the sailors despaired.

The sea continues to wash over the deck and down the stairway to the living spaces. The dry deck now covered with seawater. The 102 passengers scurry to the outside, to the ship's hull. As the ship gets thrown around, it rises to the crest of the wave.

The ship nearly capsizes, tossing the passengers on top of each other.

The heat went out with the first wave and flooded down the stairs. The 102 passengers, who were in the dark area about thirty ft. by seventy ft., with woman and children wet to the bone, are in fear of the unknown yelling, screaming throughout the night.

The waves lasted more than a day, without food. The children were chewing shoe leather; they were so hungry. Even when the water stopped coming in, the firewood was in short supply; they could only cook for every third day.

By a stroke of luck, one of the colonists had a metal jackscrew that he had purchased in Holland to help in the construction of the new settler homes. They used it to secure the beam, which kept it from cracking further, thus maintaining the seaworthiness of the vessel. All told, despite the crowding, unsanitary conditions, and sea sicknesses, there was only one fatality during the voyage. The ship's cargo included many stores that supplied the Pilgrims with the essentials needed for their journey and future lives. It is assumed that they carried tools, food, and weapons, as well as

some live animals, including dogs, sheep, goats, and poultry. The ship also held two small twenty-one-foot boats powered by oars or sails. There were also artillery pieces aboard, which they might need to defend themselves against enemy European forces or indigenous tribes.

Arrival in America

Landing of the Pilgrims (painting by Charles Lucy, c. 1898)

On November 19, 1620 (November 9, 1620), they sighted presentday Cape Cod. They spent several days trying to sail south to their planned destination of the <u>Colony of Virginia</u>, where they had obtained permission to settle from the Company of Merchant Adventurers. But the strong winter seas forced them to return to the harbor at Cape Cod hook, known today as <u>Provincetown Harbor</u>, and they set anchor on November 11.

A scouting party was sent out, and in late December, the group landed at Plymouth Harbor, where they would form the first permanent settlement of Europeans in New England. These original settlers of Plymouth Colony are known as the Pilgrim Fathers, or simply as the Pilgrims.

According to Pilgrim Hall Museum and other sources, "There are no contemporary references to the Pilgrims' landing on a rock at Plymouth." It was before setting anchor that the Mayflower Compact was drawn up and signed by the male Pilgrims and non-Pilgrim passengers (whom members of the congregation referred to as "strangers"). Among the resolutions in the Compact were those establishing legal order and to quell increasing strife within the ranks. Myles Standish was selected to make sure the rules were obeyed, as there was a consensus that discipline would need to be enforced to ensure the survival of the planned colony. Once they agreed to settle and build a self-governing community, they came ashore.https://en.wikipedia.org/wiki/Mayflower-cite_note-Rich1883- 32

The first Pilgrim baby born in America was named Peregrine—a son born on November 20, 1620, to Susanna and William White aboard the *Mayflower*, while the ship was temporarily docked in Provincetown.

The moment the Pilgrims stepped ashore was described by William Bradford, the second governor of the Plymouth Colony:

Being thus arrived in a good harbor and brought safe to land, they fell upon their knees and blessed the God of heaven, who had brought them over the vast and furious ocean, and delivered them from all the perils and miseries thereof, again to set their feet on the firm and stable earth, their proper element.

First Winter aboard Ship

Plymouth Colony was the first experiment in consensual government in Western history between individuals with one another, and not with a monarch. The colony was a mutual enterprise, not an imperial expedition organized by the Spanish or English governments. In order to survive, it depended on the consent of the colonists themselves. Necessary in order to bind the community together, it was revolutionary by chance.

—Author Rebecca Fraser

On Monday, December 7 (November 27), an exploring expedition was launched under the direction of Capt. Christopher Jones to search for a suitable settlement site.

There were thirty-four persons in the open small boat: twenty-four passengers and ten sailors. They were ill-prepared for the bitter winter weather which they encountered, as the Pilgrims were not accustomed to winter weather which was much colder than back home. They were forced to spend the night ashore due to the bad weather they encountered, ill-clad in below-freezing temperatures with wet shoes and stockings that froze overnight. Bradford wrote, "Some of our people that are dead took the original of their death here" on the expedition.

Plymouth faced many difficulties during its first winter, the most notable being the risk of starvation and the lack of suitable shelter. The Pilgrims had no way of knowing that the ground would be frozen by the middle of November, making it impossible to do any planting. Nor were they prepared for the snowstorms that would make the countryside impassable without snowshoes. And in their haste to leave, they did not think to bring any fishing rods.

From the beginning, the assistance they received from the local

Native Americans was vital. One colonist's journal reported, "We dug and found some more corn, two or three baskets full, and a bag of beans... In all we had about ten bushels, which will be enough for seed. It is with God's help that we found this corn, for how else could we have done it, without meeting some Indians who might trouble us."

Governor Bradford held out hope:

Friends, if ever we make a plantation, God works a miracle! Especially considering how scant we shall be of victuals; and, most of all, ununited amongst ourselves, and devoid of good tutors and leaders. Violence will break all. Where is the meek and humble spirit of Moses and of Nehemiah, who reedified the walls of Jerusalem, and the State of Israel?... I see not, in reason, how we shall escape, even the gasping of hungerstarved persons: but God can do much; and his will be done!

During the winter, the passengers remained onboard the *Mayflower*, suffering an outbreak of a contagious disease described as a mixture of scurvy, pneumonia, and tuberculosis. After it was over, only fifty-three passengers remained—just over half; half of the crew died as well. In the spring, they built huts ashore, and the passengers disembarked from the *Mayflower* on March 31 (March 21), 1621.

Tuberculosis's definition is "a highly variable communicable disease of humans and some other vertebrates that is caused by the tubercle bacillus and rarely in the US by a related mycobacterium (*Mycobacterium bovis*) that affects especially the lungs but may spread to other areas (such as the kidney or spinal column), and that is characterized by fever, cough, and difficulty in breathing.

Historian John Benson Lossing described that first settlement:

After many hardships, the Pilgrim Fathers first set foot December, 1620 upon a bare rock on the bleak coast of Massachusetts Bay, while all around the earth was covered with deep snow... Dreary, indeed, was the prospect before them. Exposure and privations had prostrated one half of the men before the first blow of the ax had been struck to build a habitation... One by one perished. The governor and his wife died in April 1621; and on the first of that month, forty-six of the one hundred emigrants were in their graves, nineteen of whom were signers of the Mayflower Compact.

Jones had originally planned to return to England as soon as the Pilgrims found a settlement site. But his crew members began to be ravaged by the same diseases that was befalling the Pilgrims, and he realized that he had to remain in Plymouth Harbor "till he saw his men began to recover."

The *Mayflower* lay in New Plymouth harbor through

the winter of 1620–21, then set sail for England on April 15 (April 5), 1621. As with the Pilgrims, her sailors had been decimated by disease. Jones had lost his boatswain, his gunner, three quartermasters, the cook, and more than a dozen sailors. The *Mayflower* made excellent time on her voyage back to England. The westerly winds that had buffeted her on the initial voyage pushed her along on the return trip home. She arrived in London on May 16 (May 6), 1621, less than half the time that it had taken her to sail to America.

As one of the earliest colonial vessels, the ship has become a cultural icon in the history of the United States. Celebrations for the four hundredth anniversary of the landing had been planned for 2020 in the US.

Mayflower in Plymouth Harbor

With this commemorative stamp, the US Postal Service marks the four hundredth anniversary of the arrival of the ship Mayflower in Plymouth Harbor in 1620.

The stamp's image is based on artwork of watercolor, acrylic, and gouache, a method of painting that uses opaque pigments ground in water and thickened to a glue-like consistency.

Passengers

List of Mayflower Passengers

4. Elias Story, servant of Edward Winslow

15. Ellen More, servant of Edward Winslow

16. William Brewster, separatist

17. Mary Brewster, wife

18. Love Brewster, son

19. Wrestling Brewster, son

20. Richard More, servant of William Brewster

21. Mary More, servant of William Brewster

22. Isaac Allerton, separatist

23. Mary Allerton, wife

24. Bartholomew Allerton, son

25. Remember Allerton, daughter

26. Mary Allerton, daughter

27. John Hooke, servant of Isaac Allerton

28. Miles Standish, non-separatist

29. Rose Standish, wife

30. John Alden, Mayflower crewman

31. Samuel Fuller, separatist

32. Christopher Martin, non-separatist

33. Mary Martin, wife

34. Solomon Prower, servant of Christopher Martin

35. John Langemore, servant of Christoper Martin

36. William Mullins, non-separatist

37. Alice Mullins, wife

38. Joseph Mullins, son

39. Priscilla Mullins, daughter

40. Robert Carter, servant of William Mullins

41. William White, separatist

42. Susanna White, wife

43. Resolved White, son

44. William Holbeck, servant of William White

45. Edward Thompson, servant of William White

46. Richard Warren, non-separatist

47. Stephen Hopkins, non-separatist

48. Elizabeth Hopkins, wife

49. Giles Hopkins, son

50. Constance Hopkins, daughter

51. Damaris Hopkins, daughter

52. Oceanus Hopkins, daughter born at sea

53. Edward Doten, servant of Stephen Hopkins

54. Edward Leister, servant of Stephen Hopkins

55. Edward Tilley, separatist

56. Ann Tilley, wife

57. Henry Sampson, servant of Edward Tilley

58. Humility Cooper, servant of Edward Tilley

59. John Tilley, separatist

60. Joan Tilley, wife

61. Elizabeth Tilley, daughter

62. Francis Cook, separatist

63. John Cook, son

64. Thomas Rogers, separatist

65. Joseph Rogers, son

66. Thomas Tinker, separatist

67. Wife of Thomas Tinker

68. Son of Thomas Tinker

69. John Rigsdale, non-separatist

70. Alice Rigsdale, wife

71. Edward Fuller, separatist

72. Ann Fuller, wife

73. Samuel Fuller, son

74. John Turner, separatist

75. First son of John Turner

76. Second son of John Turner

77. Francis Eaton, non-separatist

78. Sarah Eaton, wife

79. Samuel Eaton, son

80. James Chilton, separatist

81. Wife of James Chilton

82. Mary Chilton, daughter

83. John Crackstone, separatist

84. John Crackstone, son

85. John Billington, non-separatist

86. Ellen Billngton, wife

87. John Billington, son

88. Francis Billington, son

89. Moses Fletcher, separatist

90. John Goodman, separatist

91. Digory Priest, separatist

92. Thomas Williams, separatist

93. Gilbert Winslow, non-separatist

94. Edmond Margeson, non-separatist

95. Peter Brown, non-separatist

96. Richard Britteridge, non-separatist

97. Richard Clarke, non-separatist

98. Richard Gardiner, non-separatist

99. John Allerton, Mayflower crewman

100. Thomas English, Mayflower crewman

Some families traveled together, while some men came alone, leaving families in England and Leiden. More than a third of the passengers were separatists who sought to break away from the established Church of England and create a society that incorporated their own religious ideals. Other passengers were hired hands, servants, or farmers recruited by London merchants, all originally destined for the colony of Virginia.

The passengers mostly slept and lived in the low-ceilinged great cabins and on the main deck, which was seventy-five by twenty feet large (23 m × 6 m) at most. The cabins were thin-walled and extremely cramped, and the total area was twenty-five feet by fifteen feet (7.6 m × 4.5 m) at its largest.

Below decks, any person over five feet (150 cm) tall would be unable to stand up straight. The maximum possible space for each person would have been slightly less than the size of a standard single bed.

Passengers would pass the time by reading by candlelight or playing cards and games. They consumed large amounts of alcohol such as beer with meals. This was known to be safer than water, which often came from polluted sources and caused disease. No cattle or beasts of draft or burden were brought on the journey, but there were pigs, goats, and poultry.

Mayflower Ship History

There were twenty-six vessels bearing the name Mayflower in the Port Books of England during the reign of James I (1603–1625); it is not known why the name was so popular. The identity of Captain Jones's *Mayflower* is based on records from her home port, her tonnage (est. 180–200 tons), and the master's name in 1620 in order to avoid confusion with the many other Mayflower ships. It is not known when and where Mayflower was built, although late records designate her as "of London." She was designated in the port books of 1609–11 as "of Harwich" in the county of Essex, coincidentally the birthplace of Mayflower master Christopher Jones about 1570.

Records dating from August 1609 note Christopher Jones as master and part owner of *Mayflower* when his ship was chartered for a voyage from London to Trondheim in Norway and back to London. The ship lost an anchor on her return due to bad weather, and she made short delivery of her cargo of herring. Litigation resulted, and this was still proceeding in 1612. According to records, the ship was twice on the Thames at London in 1613, once in July and again in October and November, and in 1616, she was on the Thames carrying a cargo of wine, which suggests that the ship had recently been on a voyage to France, Spain, Portugal, the Canaries, or some other wine-producing land. Jones sailed *Mayflower* across the channel, taking English woolens to France and bringing French wine back to London. He also transported hats, hemp, Spanish salt, hops, and vinegar to Norway, and he may have taken *Mayflower whaling* in the North Atlantic in the Greenland area or sailed to Mediterranean ports.

After 1616, there is no further record which specifically relates to Jones's *Mayflower* until 1624. This is unusual for a ship trading to London, as it would not usually disappear from the records for such a long time. No admiralty court document can be found relating to the Pilgrim Fathers' voyage of 1620, although this might be due to the unusual way in which the transfer of the Pilgrims was arranged from Leyden to New England, or some of the records of the period might have been lost.

*****

After many hardships, the Pilgrim Fathers first set foot in December 1620 upon a bare rock on the bleak coast of Massachusetts Bay while all around the earth was covered with deep snow. Dreary, indeed, was the prospect before them. Exposure and privations had prostrated one-half of the men before the first blow of the ax had been struck to build a habitation.

Jones was one of the owners of the ship by 1620, along with Christopher Nichols, Robert Child, and Thomas Short.

It was from Child and Jones that Thomas Weston chartered her in the summer of 1620 to undertake the Pilgrim voyage. Weston had a significant role in the *Mayflower* voyage due to his membership in the Company of Merchant Adventurers, and he eventually traveled to the Plymouth Colony himself.

A boat of Pilgrim landed one day, and two members of the ships company were killed. Squanto became the peacemaker and calmed the Indian and the Pilgrim down—both were on the edge of a fullscale war.

Squanto pointed out that killing each other would not resolve anything except a lot of dead bodies. He pointed out we live on one moon, one earth, under one sky; so let's all live together. This peace landed for over fifty years.

Squanto showed the Pilgrims his fate from the past years to use the decaying huts and help the Pilgrims survive this

New England winter, while they built the new homes a short distance away.

During the heavy winter, the decaying huts were extremely fragile, and a spark would set them to blaze.

The passengers were fleeing from religious persecution by King James of England. The Mayflower Compact was the first governing document of Plymouth Colony. It was written by the male passengers of the Mayflower.

Signing of the Mayflower Compact

In the name of God, Amen. We whose names are underwritten, the loyal subjects of our dread sovereign Lord, King James, by the grace of God, of Great Britain, France and Ireland king, defender of the faith, etc., having undertaken, for the glory of God, and advancement of the Christian faith, and honor of our king and country, a voyage to plant the first colony in the Northern parts of Virginia, do by these presents solemnly and mutually in the presence of God, and one of another, covenant and combine ourselves together into a civil body politic, for our better ordering and preservation and furtherance of the ends aforesaid; and by virtue hereof to enact, constitute, and frame such just and equal laws, ordinances, acts, constitutions, and offices, from time to time, as shall be thought most meet and convenient for the general good of the colony, unto which we promise all due submission and obedience. In witness whereof we have hereunder subscribed our names at Cape-Cod the 11 of November, in the year of the reign of our sovereign lord, King James, of England, France, and Ireland the eighteenth, and of Scotland the fifty-fourth.

Anno Domini 1620. (William Brewster)

Signers of the Mayflower Compact Profiled

The 41 "True" Pilgrims Who Signed the Mayflower Compact

Alden, John. Several other families, including the Standish family, founded the town of Duxbury in the 1630s and took up residence there. He served as Duxbury's deputy to the Plymouth Court throughout the 1640s, and sat on several committees, including the Committee on Kennebec Trade, and sat on several councils of war. The love story of John Alden and Priscilla Mullins is the most famous of all the *Mayflower* Pilgrims. It has been passed down through generations and romanticized in Henry Wadsworth Longfellow's narrative poem, "The Courtship of Miles Standish."

According to historical records, Alden was twenty-one or twentytwo when he was hired as a cooper, or barrel-maker, for the voyage to America. It was his job to repair any barrels that leaked due to bad weather or had become damaged in some other way. This was important because supplies and food were stored in barrels and needed to be kept dry.

Priscilla Mullins. Eighteen years old, was a passenger on the Mayflower along with her father, mother, and brother. The family survived the journey, but her parents and brother died during the first winter.

It is historical fact that the John and Priscilla remained friends with Standish and his family. The two families left Plymouth and founded the town of Duxbury, Massachusetts. Alden's home in Duxbury was built in the early 1650s and is still standing today. They had ten children and, today, millions of Americans can trace their lineage back to this famous couple. Longfellow, himself, is a direct descendant. The Pilgrims suffered through a difficult voyage and harsh winter, but the love story between John Alden and Priscilla Mullins endured.

Allerton, Isaac. In Plymouth Colony, he was active in colony governmental affairs and business and later in trans-Atlantic trading. Problems with the latter regarding colony expenditures caused him to be censured by the colony government and ousted from the colony. Mary (Norris) Allerton was about thirty when she came on the *Mayflower* with her husband, Isaac, and three children:

Bartholomew, Remember, and Mary. Her marriage record in Leiden indicates she was from Newbury, which is presumably Newbury county In Berks, England. Searches of this area for her baptism record and other Norris family records have not yet turned up anything conclusive. They buried a child at St. Peters, Leiden, on 5 February 1620, and she gave birth to a stillborn son in Plymouth Harbor on December 22, 1620. She herself died during the height of the first winter, on February 25, 1620, though her husband and three children all survived.

Allerton, John was a seaman who arrived as a member of the company. He was meant to return to Europe with the *Mayflower* but died in the first winter before April 5, 1621. He signed the Mayflower Compact. He was likely the brother of Isaac Allerton.

There are many notable figures in the *Mayflower* story, but few people played a bigger role in establishing Plymouth Colony than Isaac Allerton.

During his time in England and Holland, Allerton was a humble tailor—but all that was to change when he boarded the ship in Plymouth in September 1620.

Although he and his family survived the treacherous transatlantic crossing, Allerton then had to suffer the unimaginable grief of losing his wife and newborn child while the *Mayflower* was anchored off Cape Cod.

Despite his personal tragedy, Allerton went on to become one of the Pilgrims' leading figures, as well as protecting his children so they could grow up to have families of their own.

He served the colony's elected governors for more than a decade and later became an influential businessman and politician.

Bradford, William. Although not educated at one university,

Bradford could certainly hold his own with any of those who were. His library was one of the most extensive among the first generation of New Englanders. Like many of the ministers; he had knowledge of many loan languages, including Hebrew. His education was also on display in his writings

William Bradford explains, in chapter 6 of the book, that the reason he wrote the manuscript was so that the descendants of the Pilgrims would know and appreciate the hardships their ancestors faced:

I have been ye larger in these things, and so shall crave leave in some passages following, (though in other things I shall labour to be more contract,) that their children may see with what difficulties their fathers wrestled in going through these things in their first beginings, and how God brought them, along notwithstanding all their weakness and infirmities. As also that some use may be made hereof in after times by others in such like weighty employments; and herewith I will end this chapter. (History of Plimoth Plantation p. 58).

Bradford never made any attempt to publish the manuscript during his lifetime and instead gave it to his son, William, who later passed it on to his own son, Major John Bradford.

Brewster, William. In Leiden, Brewster worked with Thomas Brewer, Edward Winslow, and others and began working a printing press and publishing religious books and pamphlets that were then illegally conveyed into England

Brewster, along with Robinson, was a prime mover in the decision to sail for North America and a principal organizer, but once he was in hiding, the separatists looked to their deacon, John Carver, and to Robert Cushman to carry on negotiations with the appropriate officials in London. In 1620, when it came time for the *Mayflower* departure, Brewster returned to the Leiden congregation. He had been hiding out in Holland and perhaps even England for the last year. At the time of his return, Brewster was the highest-ranking layperson of the congregation and would be their designated spiritual leader in the New World.

Brewster joined the first group of separatists aboard the Mayflower on the voyage to North America. Brewster was accompanied by his wife, Mary Brewster, and his sons, Love Brewster and Wrestling Brewster.

The *Mayflower* departed Plymouth in England in September 1620. The hundred-foot vessel carried 102 passengers and a crew of thirty to forty in extremely cramped conditions. During the voyage, the ship was buffeted by strong westerly gales. The caulking of its planks was failing to keep out seawater, and the passengers' berths were not always dry. On the journey, there were two deaths, a crew member and a passenger. After being blown off course by gales, the *Mayflower* made a landing at Cape Cod. Finding the area near Provincetown occupied by Indigenous people, the ship's company decided to continue exploring along the nearby coast. The group arrived in the area near present-day Plymouth, Massachusetts on December 21, 1620. In the space of several months, almost half the passengers perished in the cold, harsh New England winter.

Billington, John was a Mayflower Pilgrim and a signer of the Mayflower Compact, who became America's first murderer after he shot and killed a fellow colonist in 1630. Billington was born in England about 1582. In 1603, he married a woman named Elinor Lockwood and had two sons: John, who was born in 1604, and Francis, who was born about 1606.

John Billington's story is as a boy of the *Mayflower*

whose natural mistakes were often interpreted unjustly as carelessness and open aggression, but his friendship for Squanto provided the means for a wider friendship between his people and the Indians of Cape Cod. After the Pilgrims settled, John is made especially miserable by the current misunderstanding and runs off.

Squanto was a member of the Patuxet tribe best known for being an early liaison between the Native American population in Southern New England and the Mayflower Pilgrims who made their settlement at the site of Tisquantum's.

John Crackstone, from Leiden, Holland. Migration: 1620 on Mayflower. First residence: Plymouth. Birth: No later than about 1575 based on marriage of daughter. Death: Plymouth, between January 11, 1620/1 and 10 April 1621. Married by about 1600, wife unknown, and probably dead by 1620 and perhaps considerably earlier. A child Anna was married in Leiden. He was among the signers of the Mayflower Compact.

Carver, John. Separatist was one of the Pilgrims who braved the Mayflower voyage in 1620, which resulted in the creation of Plymouth Colony in America. He is credited with writing the Mayflower Compact and was its first signer, and he was also the firs governor of Plymouth Colony.

Carver and his wife, Katherine, boarded *Mayflower* with five servants and seven-year-old Jasper More, one of the four children of the More family who were sent in the care of the Pilgrims. Carver seems to have been elected governor of the *Mayflower* for the duration of the Atlantic crossing. The Mayflower anchored off Cape Cod in November 1620, and the Mayflower Compact was signed aboard ship on November 11; it became the first governing document for Plymouth Colony. Carver may have been the author of the Compact and was definitely its first signer. He was subsequently chosen to be governor of Plymouth Colony.

Chilton, James was born in England around 1556. He was a resident of Canterbury. James Chilton was part of the Pilgrim separatist community in Leiden. In 1620, he journeyed to

Plymouth on the *Mayflower* with his wife and daughter, Mary. James Chilton died before the *Mayflower* reached Plymouth.

The one at the Winthrop Street Cemetery is pictured as the plaque on the fenced-in rock. The other one is the Mayflower Passengers Who Died at Sea memorial, which is at Bradford Street at Ryder Street in the park. If you put the Provincetown Hall at your back and see the Pilgrim monument looming over you, then look down to the ground and to the left. The memorial resembles a tall gravestone and is a great photo spot!

Cooke, Francis, and his oldest son, John, came on the *Mayflower* to Plymouth in 1620. He left behind his wife, Hester, and his other children, Jane, Jacob, Elizabeth, and Hester. After the colony was founded and better established, he sent for his wife and children, and they came to Plymouth.

Francis lived out his life in Plymouth. Although he kept a fairly low profile, he was on a number of minor committees such as the committee to lay out the highways and received some minor appointments by the court to survey land. He was a juror on a number of occasions and was on the coroner's jury that examined the body of Martha Bishop, the four-year-old daughter who was murdered by her mother, Alice. He received some modest land grants at various times throughout his life. He lived to be about eighty years old, dying in 1663. His wife, Hester, survived him by at least three years and perhaps longer.

Edward Doty came on the *Mayflower* in 1620 as a servant to Stephen Hopkins and was apparently still a servant in 1623 when the Division of Land was held, indicating he was under the age of twenty-five during that time. He signed the Mayflower Compact in November 1620, so he was likely over twenty-one at the time. This narrows his likely birth date to around 1597–1599. Doty had a lot of spunk and energy. He made the decision to take the Mayflower voyage.

Edward Liseter. Edward Leister was one of two servants, or apprentices, brought by Mayflower passenger Stephen Hopkins. Since he was a signer of the Mayflower Compact, we can assume he was over eighteen or twenty-one years of age, but as a servant, he was almost certainly under the age of twenty-five. This would place his birth at somewhere between 1595 and 1602.

He, along with fellow servant Edward Doty, proved to be somewhat on the rowdy side. They were the last two men to sign the Mayflower Compact, which has led some to speculate they may have been originally unwilling to sign and required some persuasion. In June 1621, the two servants would engage in a duel, both wounding each other before the fight was broken up. They were sentenced by the company to have their head and feet tied together for a full day, but the sentence was commuted after an hour due to their apparent suffering and the plea of their master, Stephen Hopkins, for their release.

Leister was enumerated in the 1623 division of land but disappears by the time of the 1627 division of cattle. William Bradford indicates that as soon as his contract was up, he headed off to Jamestown, where he later died.

English, Thomas. Very little is known about *Mayflower* passenger Thomas English beyond his name and the fact he died sometime in the first winter at Plymouth, probably between January and March 1621.

Fuller, Samuel. His traditionally reported baptism of January 20, 1580, was recently corrected upon review of the original parish registers. The baptism date was actually February 20, 1580/1.

Samuel Fuller has been generally identified as the son of Robert Fuller, baptized on February 20, 1580/1, at Redenhall county, Norfolk. The identification is based upon circumstantial evidence only: the fact that the names Samuel, Edward, and Ann occur within the same family, and the fact the father is identified as a butcher. Thomas Morton, writing in 1637, says that Samuel Fuller was the son of a butcher. The name Matthew also occurs in this Redenhall Fuller family.

Samuel Fuller's 1613 Leiden marriage record indicates

he had been formerly married to Alice Glascock; nothing is known of his first wife beyond her name. The name Alice Glascock is found most commonly in the county Of Essex, England. His second wife, Agnes Carpenter, was the daughter of Alexander Carpenter. She was baptized at Wrington, Somerset, on December 16, 1593. His third wife, Bridget Lee, was accompanied by her mother, Josephine Lee, at her marriage and also had a brother Samuel Lee living in Leiden.

Samuel Fuller came on the *Mayflower* in 1620, leaving behind his wife, Bridget. She would come later, on the ship *Anne* in 1623. He was the colony's doctor and was a church deacon. His wife, Bridget, may have been the church's deaconess. Samuel Fuller spent time helping the sick at Neumkeag (now Salem) in 1629. He himself became sick in the autumn of 1633 and died, as did a number of other Plymouth residents.

Francis Eaton. The burial place of his first wife, Sarah, is unknown, but most likely her burial was in an unmarked grave on Coles Hill, the first Pilgrim burial location, as with so many others who died in the first winter of 1621. The reason for the unmarked graves was so that the Native Americans would not know how decimated their numbers were, with so many deaths. She is memorialized on the Pilgrim Memorial Tomb (Sarcophagus) on Cole's Hill in Plymouth with "Sarah."

Fuller Edward was born in England and sailed with the Pilgrims from Leiden, traveling with his wife and son, Samuel. He was married around 1605, although the name of his wife is unknown. Both Edward and his wife died during the first winter in January 1621.

The name of Edward Fuller's wife has not been discovered. In James Savage's *Genealogical Dictionary of the First Settlers of New England (1860–1862)*, Edward Fuller's wife was given as "Ann." However, there are no American or English records which give her name. I suspect James Savage may have made a simple typographical error. *Mayflower* passenger Edward Tilley had a wife, Ann, or perhaps he was thinking of their sister Ann Fuller. Nonetheless, numerous sources published after 1860 have utilized Savage's *Genealogical Dictionary*, and so the identification of Ann can be found in numerous other books and online resources.

Very little is known about Edward Fuller. What is known is that he, his wife, and his son Samuel came on the *Mayflower* in 1620 to Plymouth. An older brother, Matthew, had stayed behind, and came to America later.

Goodman, John. Governor William Bradford, in his otherwise nearly flawless recitation of *Mayflower* passengers made in 1651, states that John Goodman was one of those who "died soon after their arrival in the general sickness that befell."

John Goodman has been a difficult *Mayflower* passenger to research. Governor William Bradford, in his otherwise nearly flawless recitation of *Mayflower* passengers made in 1651, states that John Goodman was one of those who "died soon after their arrival in the general sickness that befell." However, that is contradicted by his appearance on the 1623 division of land, where he received an acre of land. In any case, Goodman had disappeared by the time of the 1627 division of cattle, and presumably died very early on.

In 1905, Henry Martyn Dexter proposed that John Goodman was the man found in Leiden records as John "Codmoer," widower of Mary Backus, who married Sarah Hooper. But this has been disputed by many later researchers as unfounded: "Codmoer" is a pretty significant misspelling of "Goodman" even by Dutch standards. To further complicate the situation, there is an oft-published hoax that surfaced in the nineteenth century that John Goodman was actually a pseudonym for John Dunham, another member of the Leiden congregation. However, this has been conclusively disproven; John Dunham was still living in Leiden after the *Mayflower's* departure.

On January 12, 1621, Peter Browne and John Goodman were cutting thatch for house roofing and went for a short walk to refresh themselves when their mastiff and spaniel spied a deer and gave chase. Peter and John soon found themselves lost. They spent the night in a tree, in rain and snow, because they thought they heard a lion. They found their way back to Plymouth the following day. Goodman suffered some frostbite. When he was finally able to walk, he took his spaniel out and found himself being followed by a wolf. After a long stare-down and having securing a fence post for defense, the wolf eventually departed.

Howland, John was one of the forty-one "true" <u>Pilgrims</u> who signed <u>the Mayflower Compact</u>, and in 1624 he married fellow Mayflower passenger <u>Elizabeth Tilley</u>, daughter of John and Joan Tilley. The couple had ten children, who all survived into adulthood.

Hopkins, Stephen. This is the story of Stephen Hopkins, a *settler* among the Pilgrims during his second trip to the New World. He was in Virginia in 1615 when he received the news that his wife had died and his children needed their father. He went to England, picked up the children and as much possessions as they had, and remarried.

Martin, Christopher. On the historic 1620 voyage of the Pilgrim ship Mayflower on its journey to the New World, he was initially the governor of passengers on the ship *Speedwell* until that ship was found to be unseaworthy, and later on the *Mayflower*, until replaced by John Carver. He was a signatory to the Mayflower Compact.

Fletcher, Moses. Moses Fletcher was born in 1565 in Sandwich, Kent, England. He was approximately fifty-five years old when he sailed on the *Mayflower*. Moses came with the members of the Leiden congregation from Holland.

Mullins, William. One man who made a telling financial contribution to the famous voyage was William Mullins. The year before the *Mayflower* set sail, Mullins made one of the largest investments in the Pilgrims' joint stock company and subsequently—and rather unusually—went on to become one of the ship's passengers.

Margeson, Edmund. Edward Margeson came on the

Mayflower as an adult by himself. He signed the Mayflower Compact. Other than the fact he died sometime the first winter, likely between January and March 1621, nothing else is known about him. A search of baptism records in England has identified one potential candidate, an Edmund Margetson baptized on November 23, 1586, at Swannington county, Norfolk, son of Robert. However, with no other supporting details beyond a name, nothing conclusive can be determined beyond he came to Plymouth in 1620 on the *Mayflower* and "died soon after...arrival in the general sickness" and "left no posterity here."

Browne, Peter may have heard of the proposed *Mayflower* voyage from his relationship with the Mullins family. William Mullins was a shoe- and bootmaker in Dorking and was one of the Londoners who was later involved in the financial support of the *Mayflower* voyage About a year later, Peter and Martha would have daughter Priscilla (perhaps named after *Mayflower* passenger Priscilla Mullins who was also from Dorking), but wife Martha would die shortly thereafter. Peter was remarried to a woman named Mary, whose maiden name has not been discovered. With her, he had a daughter, Rebecca, born about 1631, and another child who was born about 1633 and died before reaching adulthood (the name of this child has not been discovered).

Peter Browne died in 1633, probably during the general sickness that occurred that autumn and also killed neighbor Samuel Fuller, *Mayflower* passenger Francis Eaton, and several others in Plymouth. His estate inventory, taken October 10, 1633, shows that he owned 130 bushels of corn, six male goats, one cow, eight sheep, and a number of pigs, among other things. Peter Browne and his brothers were all weavers, which explains why he had more sheep than anyone else in Plymouth at the time.

Priest, Degory (c. 1579–c. 1621) and wife Sarah had two children, Mary and Sarah. Degory came alone on the *Mayflower*, planning to bring wife and children later after the colony was better established. His death the first winter ended those plans. His wife was remarried

to Godbert Godbertson in Leiden on November 13, 1621, and they had a son Samuel together. Godbert, his wife Sarah, their son Samuel, and his stepchildren Mary and Sarah Priest all came on the ship Anne to Plymouth in 1623. He was a member of the **Leiden** contingent on the historic 1620 voyage of the ship *Mayflower*. He was a hat maker from London who married Sarah, sister of Pilgrim Isaac Allerton in Leiden. He was a signatory to the Mayflower Compact in November 1620 and died less than two months later.

Rigsdale, John. Nothing much is known about John and Alice Rigsdale, other than the fact they both came on the Mayflower and they both died at some time during the first winter at Plymouth, probably between January and March 1621. There is a marriage record of a John Rigsdale and an Alice Gallard at St. Mary, Weston county, Lincoln, England on November 17, 1577.

Standish, Myles (c. 1584–October 3, 1656) was an English military officer. He was hired as military adviser for Plymouth Colony in present-day Massachusetts, United States, by the Pilgrims. Standish accompanied the Pilgrims on the ship *Mayflower* and played a leading role in the administration and defense of Plymouth Colony from its foundation in 1620.

Miles Standish was a member of Queen Elizabeth's army. The Pilgrims hired him to be in charge of military operations, protecting the colony against threats from the French, Dutch, Spanish, and Native Americans. He and his first wife, Rose, survived the voyage, but she died that first winter.

Longfellow's poem opens with the Pilgrims already at Plymouth. That first winter is over, and Captain Standish tells Alden that, since his wife died, he wants to remarry. He asks Alden to speak to the woman on his behalf, claiming that he knows what to say in battle but finds it difficult to propose marriage. Alden agrees but is surprised to hear the woman's name is Priscilla, the same one he has been admiring for months. He goes to her home and offers the proposal in the name of Standish, but her response is, "Why don't you speak for yourself, John?"

Standish is in a rage after hearing what happened and accuses Alden of betrayal. He cuts his tirade short, though, when he receives word about an Indian revolt. While he is off fighting, the *Mayflower* departs Plymouth for England.

Tilley, Edward (c. 1588–c. winter of 1620/1621). Edward Tilley was born in 1588 in Henlow county, Bedford, England, the son of Robert and Elizabeth Tilley. He married Agnes Cooper on June 20, 1614, in Henlow. Shortly after their marriage, they moved to Leiden, Holland, where he is recorded in a notary record dated April 25, 1618. They came on the *Mayflower* along with their niece and nephew Humility Cooper and Henry Samson. Edward signed the Mayflower Compact and participated in the early explorations on Cape Cod, where he was once appointed to provide "advice and council" to Myles Standish. By the time of the third exploration at Cape Cod, Edward Tilley had developed a cold. He would later die the first winter at Plymouth traveled in 1620.

Tilley, John joined the expedition of December 6, 1620, along the coast with nine others, under the leadership of Miles Standish (Young's Pilgrim Fathers).

Hurst, Joan. Joan Hurst was born in 1567/8 in Henlow, Bedford, England, the daughter of William and Rose Hurst. She married first to Thomas Rogers in 1593 (not related to the *Mayflower* passenger Thomas Rogers). With her husband Thomas, she had a daughter Joan, baptized on May 26, 1594, in Henlow. Attempts to determine what happened to Joan have so far been unsuccessful. She may have died young. When her first husband Thomas died, likely around 1594 or 1595, she remarried to John Tilly.

John and Joan (Hurst and Rogers) Tilley came on the *Mayflower* in 1620, bringing with them daughter *Elizabeth*. Joan, along with her husband, died the first winter at Plymouth, orphaning their thirteenyear old daughter Elizabeth in the

New World. Elizabeth would later marry Mayflower passenger John Howland.

Winslow, Edward (born October 18, 1595, Droitwich, Worcestershire, England, and died May 8, 1655, at sea, near Jamaica, British West Indies), English founder of the Plymouth colony in Massachusetts. Edward Winslow was born in Droitwich county, Worcester, in 1595. He was traveling in the Low Countries and subsequently became acquainted with the Pilgrims' church in Leiden. He was married in Leiden in 1618 to Elizabeth Barker and was called a printer of London at the time. He had been apprenticed to London printer John Beale in 1613, and it is quite possible he was assisting William Brewster and Thomas Brewer in their publication and distribution of religious books that were illegal in England.

Edward Winslow and his wife, Elizabeth, came on the *Mayflower* to Plymouth in 1620. Elizabeth died the first winter, and Edward remarried to the widowed Susanna (Jackson) White, on May 12, 1621—the first marriage in the Plymouth Colony.

Winslow quickly became one of the more prominent men in the colony. He was on many of the early explorations of Cape Cod and led a number of expeditions to meet and trade with the Indians. He wrote several firsthand accounts of these early years, including portions of *A Relation or Journal of the Proceedings of the Plantation Settled at Plymouth* (London, 1622) and the entirety of *Good News from New England* (London, 1624).

A mortar and pestle that is believed to have been owned by Edward Winslow is on display at the Pilgrim Hall Museum in Plymouth.

Edward Winslow became involved in defending the Plymouth and later Massachusetts Bay colonies from their opponents and adversaries in England and made several trips back and forth between England and Massachusetts, including trips in 1623/4, 1630, and 1634. On one occasion, he was arrested and thrown into the Fleet Prison in London by his adversaries, on grounds that he had performed marriage ceremonies without being ordained (the Pilgrims viewed marriage as an event to be handled by the civil magistrates, not by the church).

Winslow returned to England shortly after the English Civil War and published a couple of pamphlets in defense of the New England colonies, including *Hypocrisy Unmasked* (1646) and *New England's Salamander Discovered* (1647). He also wrote the introduction to the *Glorious Progress of the Gospel Amongst the Indians in New England* (1649).

In Plymouth, he held a number of political offices, as he was routinely elected an assistant to Governor William Bradford. Winslow himself was elected governor of Plymouth on three occasions: 1632/3, 1635/6, and 1644. After Winslow returned to England, he was on several parliamentary committees. He died in 1655 at sea between Hispaniola and Jamaica, while serving as a commissioner for Oliver Cromwell on a military expedition to retake the island of Hispaniola.

White, William (c. 1572–1621) and his family traveled as passengers on the historic 1620 voyage to America on the Pilgrim ship *Mayflower*. He was a signatory to the Mayflower Compact. Mullins perished in the Pilgrims' first winter in the New World, with his wife and son dying soon after.

Warren, Richard. Richard Warren, was a passenger on the *Mayflower*, arriving in Plymouth in 1620. We know he was from London, and the evidence seems to indicate that he was a man of some wealth. His wife, Elizabeth, arrived in Plymouth on the *Anne* in 1623 with the couples' daughters Abigail, Anna, Elizabeth, Mary and Sarah. Two sons, Nathaniel and Joseph, were born to the Warrens in Plymouth.

Thomas Rogers (c. 1571–January 11, 1621) was a Leiden separatist who traveled in 1620 with his eldest son, Joseph, as passengers on the historic voyage of the Pilgrim ship *Mayflower*. Thomas Rogers was a signatory to the *Mayflower* Compact but perished in the winter of 1620/21. His son, Joseph, who at the age of seventeen had traveled with

Thomas on the Mayflower had been too young to sign.

Tinker, Thomas. Thomas Tinker and his family, comprising his wife and son, came in 1620 as English separatists from Holland on the historic voyage of the Pilgrim ship the *Mayflower*. He was a signatory to the Mayflower Compact, but he and his family all perished in the winter of 1620/1621, described by Bradford as having died in "the first sickness."

Turner, John was a passenger, along with his two sons, on the 1620 voyage of the historic Pilgrim ship the *Mayflower*. He was a signatory to the Mayflower Compact and perished with his sons that first winter. Little is known about John Turner and his family—even the names of his two sons that came on the *Mayflower* remain unknown.

They all died in the first winter at Plymouth, likely between January and March 1621. John Turner was a merchant living in Leiden and was granted citizenship there on September 27, 1610, making him one of the earliest members of the Pilgrim congregation to get his citizenship there. On June 11, 1620, the Pilgrims' business agent and fellow church member Robert Cushman wrote a letter saying, "I received your letter yesterday, by John Turner" and later wrote "You shall hear distinctly by John Turner, who I think shall come hence on Tuesday night." This suggests Turner was traveling between England and Holland. Unfortunately, there are far too many men named John Turner living in England for there to be any hope of identifying further details.

John Turner had a daughter named Elizabeth who remained behind in Holland, came to New England later, and married there— perhaps in Salem. Unfortunately, her identity has not been discovered, and with a common name like Elizabeth, it will be extraordinarily difficult to do so with any level of certainty.

Williams, Thomas came to Plymouth in 1620 on the *Mayflower* and signed the Mayflower Compact. He died soon after arrival in the general sickness (Thomas Williams and his sister Elizabeth, who did not come on the *Mayflower*, are found in the records of Leiden, Holland, and belonged to the Pilgrims' church congregation there). On March 11, 1616, Thomas witnessed his sister's marriage to fellow church member Roger Wilson, and in this record they are said to have originally come from Great Yarmouth, Norfolk, England. The parish registers of Great Yarmouth show Thomas's baptism on August 12, 1582, as well as his sister Elizabeth's on January 9, 1591/2.

Winslow, Gilbert, who was one of the first comers to have a right of land and to allow his heirs to look out and propose to the court some parcel of land that the court may think accommodate them. Gilbert Winslow was twenty years old when he came on the *Mayflower* with his older brother Edward Winslow. Other brothers Kenelm, John, and Josiah, also later came to New England.

Gilbert signed the Mayflower Compact in November 1620. William Bradford recorded that Gilbert Winslow lived in Plymouth for "divers years" before he "returned into England and died there." Since Gilbert is not recorded in the 1627 division of cattle at Plymouth, he had likely left by then.

Gilbert's burial and probate administration, which occurred in 1631, were only recently discovered at Ludlow, Shropshire, England, where his estate was valued at just over £30. It was administered by his brother Edward.

In 1663, the Plymouth court acknowledged Gilbert Winslow, deceased, was a first-comer and his heirs could seek out and purpose a plot of land to the court. The estate inventory of Kenelm Winslow, another brother who came to New England later, mentions that he and his brother John were granted Gilbert Winslow's land.

Clarke, Richard. Almost nothing is known about *Mayflower* passenger Richard Clarke. He is enumerated by William Bradford on the *Mayflower* passenger list in a way that suggests he was an adult. He died the first winter at Plymouth, leaving no descendants. The Clarke surname is far too common to do any serious research in England, so there is little hope of ever discovering or learning anything further about this passenger.

Gardiner, Richard. Origins are uncertain. He may have been the man baptized February 12, 1582, at Harwich, Essex, England, into a family that was associated with *Mayflower* master Christopher Jones. Or he may have been the Richard Gardinar of Holy Trinity, Guildford, Surrey, whose family appears to have ties to *Mayflower* passenger William Mullins.

Soule, George. It is known that George came on the Mayflower and was credited to the household of Edward Winslow as a manservant or apprentice, along with Elias Story and a little girl, Ellen More, who both died in the first winter.

George was orphaned when fire destroyed his home. He was brought up by his brother, Robert Soule of Selter county. He came to America on the *Mayflower* and was a signer of the Mayflower pact. He came as a teacher to Edward Winsow's children. Mary Beckett came on the *Anne*, and they were married in Plymouth. George Soule, Miles Standish, and John Alden laid out the first town, Duxbury, and are buried there.

He has been tentatively identified as son of John Soule of Eckington, Worcester, and probably kinsman to Robert Soule, a wealthy London salter who died in 1590, a native of Eckington. Robert Soule had a son Miles and a grandson of George, the emigrant who also bore that name. All other George Soules found in England at that period have been satisfactorily eliminated. Fuller particulars of this identification will be found in the recently published Soule genealogy for which a special extensive search covering a number of years was made by the compiler of this book.

The Winslow family from which Edward was descended lived in the nearby parish of Kempsey, Worcester, and it is probable that this early neighborhood association explains the apprenticeship of George Soule to the governor. It is supposed that George Soule was in London when he joined Winslow on the voyage. Droitwich, the family home of the Winslow's at that time, was a salt mining place connected in a business way with the Salters' company of London in trade, and thus the Winslow-Soule association was established. The name of Mary Bucket, his wife, who came in the Anne, should be looked for in the parish of St. Botolph, Aldersgate, London. It is probably a variation of Beckett. The marriage is established through the sale by George Soule of that acre of land granted to her as a passenger, which he could do as her husband, deputy to general court, Duxbury, Massachusetts.

Women of Early Plymouth

Governor William Bradford reported that the Pilgrims were worried that the "weak bodies of women" would not be able to withstand the rigors of a transatlantic voyage and the construction of a colony. Prior to the *Mayflower*, very few English women had made the voyage across the ocean. Sir Walter Raleigh's Roanoke colony arrived in Virginia in 1587, and among those 120 colonists, there were seventeen women. A baby girl, Virginia Dare, was born after arrival. When resupply ships came from England, they could not relocate the people. The colony had mysteriously disappeared and was never seen again. The Jamestown Colony was founded in 1607, but relatively few women had yet made the voyage and taken up residence there.

The Pilgrim husband, as head of the household, had an important and difficult decision to make. Building a colony would be hard on a woman's "weaker body." It might be safer and healthier to leave her behind and have her come later once the houses were built, and the general safety and successfulness of the colony were better established. But that could be several years. Could he live several years without his wife? How strong was his wife anyway? Could she really handle it? Was it right to put your wife's life in danger in this manner?

Francis Cooke, Thomas Rogers, Samuel Fuller, and Richard Warren felt it was better if their wives Hester, Alice, Bridget, and Elizabeth stayed behind and came over later. Degory Priest also left behind his wife Sarah, despite the fact that Sarah's brother Isaac Allerton came on the *Mayflower* with his pregnant wife and three young children. But most husbands, eighteen in total, decided their wives should come with them. Was it the right decision?

As the *Mayflower* left England for America, there were eighteen adult women on-board. Three of them, Elizabeth Hopkins, Susanna White, and Mary Allerton were actually in their last trimester of a pregnancy. All the adult women on the *Mayflower* were married; there were no single women—although there were a few teenage girls nearing marriageable age.

While no women would die during the *Mayflower*'s voyage, life after arrival proved extremely difficult. In fact, 78 percent of the women would die the first winter, a far higher percentage than for men or children. Dorothy Bradford was the first woman to die, and the only woman who died in the month of December. While many of the men, including her husband, were out exploring on Cape Cod, she accidentally fell off the *Mayflower* into the bitter cold waters of Provincetown Harbor. Most of the women's death dates were not recorded, but we do know that Rose Standish died on January 29, Mary Allerton died on February 25, and Elizabeth Winslow died on March 24. Most of the women died in February and March.

The extremely high mortality rate among women is probably explainable by the fact the men were out in the fresh air, felling trees, building structures, and drinking fresh New England water, while the women were confined to the damp, filthy, and crowded quarters offered by the *Mayflower,* where disease would have spread much more quickly. The two-month voyage was long enough; the women, however, remained living on the ship for an additional four months

while the men built storehouses and living quarters on shore. Many of the sick were no doubt cared for onboard the ship by the women, increasing their exposure to colds and pneumonias. William Mullins died on February 21, apparently onboard the *Mayflower* since his will was witnessed by the ship's captain and ship's surgeon. His wife, Alice, and son, Joseph, had not yet died, but it wasn't too long before they did, orphaning their teenage daughter, Priscilla, in the New World.

Only five women survived the first winter. One of the five survivors, Mrs. Katherine Carver, died in May of a "broken heart," her husband John having died of sunstroke a month earlier. Weak bodies or not, by the time of the famous "Thanksgiving," there were only four women left to care for the colony's fifty surviving men and children. The four women were Eleanor Billington, Elizabeth Hopkins, Mary Brewster, and Susanna (White) Winslow. Susanna Winslow was the widow of William White who died the first winter; she remarried to Edward Winslow, whose wife Elizabeth had also died the first winter.

Incidentally, all the wives who had been left behind were still living. Four of them came on the ship *Anne* in 1623, had additional children, and raised their families at Plymouth.

The settlement served as the capital of the colony and developed as the town of *Plymouth, Massachusetts*. At its height, Plymouth Colony occupied most of the southeastern portion of Massachusetts. Plymouth Colony was founded by a group of Puritan separatists initially known as the Brownist Emigration, who came to be known as the Pilgrims.

Later History

Three of *Mayflower*'s owners applied to the admiralty court for an appraisal of the ship on May 4, 1624, two years after Captain Jones's death in 1622. One of these applicants was Jones's widow, Mrs. Josian (Joan) Jones. This appraisal probably was made to determine the valuation of the ship for the purpose of settling the estate of its late master. The appraisal was made by four mariners and shipwrights of Rotherhithe, home and burial place of Captain Jones, where *Mayflower* was apparently then lying in the Thames at London. The appraisement is extant and provides information on the ship's gear onboard at that time, as well as equipment such as muskets and other arms. The ship may have been laid up since Jones's death and allowed to get out of repair as that is what the appraisal indicates. The vessel was valued at 128 pounds, eight shillings, and four pence.

What finally became of *Mayflower* is an unsettled issue. Charles Edward Banks, an English historian of the Pilgrim ship, claims that the ship was finally broken up, with her timbers used in the construction of a barn at *Jordans* village in *Buckinghamshire*. Tradition claims that this barn still exists as the *Mayflower Barn*, located within the grounds of Old Jordan in South Buckinghamshire. In 1624, Thomas Russell supposedly added to part of a farmhouse already there with timbers from a ship, believed to be from the Pilgrim ship *Mayflower*, bought from a ship-breaker's yard in Rotherhithe. The well-preserved structure was a tourist attraction, receiving visitors each year from all over the world and particularly from America, but it is now privately owned and not open to the public.

Second Mayflower

Another ship called *Mayflower* made a voyage from London to Plymouth Colony in 1629, carrying thirty-five passengers, many from the Pilgrim congregation in <u>Leiden</u> that organized the first voyage. This was not the same ship that made the original voyage with the first settlers. The 1629 voyage began in May and reached Plymouth in August; this ship also made the crossing from England to America in 1630 (as part of the <u>Winthrop Fleet</u>), 1633, 1634, and 1639. It attempted the trip again in 1641, departing London in October of that year under master John Cole, with 140 passengers bound for Virginia. It never arrived. On October 18, 1642, a deposition was made in England regarding the loss.

Mayflower structure and layout Mayflower Officers, Crew, and Others

According to author Charles Banks, the officers and crew of *Mayflower* consisted of a captain, four mates, four quartermasters, surgeon, carpenter, cooper, cooks, boatswains, gunners, and about thirty-six men before the mast, making a total of about fifty. The entire crew stayed with the *Mayflower* in Plymouth through the winter of 1620–1621, and about half of them died during that time. The remaining crewmen returned to England on the *Mayflower*, which sailed for London on April 15 (April 5), 1621.

Legacy

Mayflower Tercentenary stamp, 1920

The Pilgrim ship *Mayflower* has a famous place in American history as a symbol of early European colonization of the future United States. As described by the European *History* channel:

Out of all the voyages to the American colonies from 1620 to 1640, the *Mayflower*'s first crossing of Pilgrim Fathers has become the most culturally iconic and important in the history of migration from Europe to the New World during the Age of Discovery.

Plymouth Plantation

Plymouth Plantation Village

The main record for the voyage of *Mayflower* and the disposition of the Plymouth Colony comes from the letters and journal of William Bradford, who was a guiding force and later the governor of the colony. His detailed record of the journey is one of the primary sources used by historians, and the most complete history of Plymouth Colony that was written by a *Mayflower* passenger.

The First Thanksgiving at Plymouth by Jennie A. Brownscombe (1914)

The American national holiday, Thanksgiving, originated from the first Thanksgiving feast held by the Pilgrims in 1621, a prayer event and dinner to mark the first harvest of the *Mayflower* settlers.

Three Hundred Anniversaries

The three hundredth anniversary of the *Mayflower*'s landing was commemorated in 1920 and early 1921 by celebrations throughout the United States and by countries in Europe. Delegations from England, Holland, and Canada met in New York. The mayor of New York, John Francis Hylan, in his speech, said that the principles of the Pilgrim's Mayflower Compact were precursors to the United States Declaration of Independence. While American historian George Bancroft called it "the birth of constitutional liberty." Governor Calvin Coolidge similarly credited the forming of the compact as an event of the greatest importance in American history: It was the foundation of liberty based on law and order, and that tradition has been steadily upheld. They drew up a form of government which has been designated as the first real constitution of modern times. It was democratic, an acknowledgment of liberty under law and order and the giving to each person the right to participate in the government, while they promised to be obedient to the laws. Any form of government is better than anarchy, and any attempt to tear down government is an attempt to wreck civilization.

https://en.wikipedia.org/wiki/File:Pilgrim_tercentenary_half_dollar_commemorative_reverse.

jpg

Mayflower tercentenary half dollar

With twenty *Mayflower* historical societies throughout the country, along with an unknown number of descendants, the celebration was expected to last during much of 1920. As a result of World War I ending a few years earlier, the original plan to hold a world's fair in its honor was canceled. The government issued a Pilgrim tercentenary half-dollar, which portrays the ship on its reverse and passenger William Bradford on its obverse.

The Story of Thanksgiving

But some historians argue that Florida, not Massachusetts, may have been the true site of the first Thanksgiving in North America. In 1565, nearly sixty years before Plymouth, a Spanish fleet came ashore and planted a cross in the sandy beach to christen the new settlement of St. Augustine. To celebrate the arrival and give thanks for God's providence, the eight hundred Spanish settlers shared a festive meal with the native Timucuan people.

"The Timucua ate what was available to them locally and that could have included alligator, bear, wild turkey, venison, tortoise and food from the sea such as turtle, shark, mullet or sea catfish," Gioia says. Archaeological research also shows the Indigenous people ate large amounts of oysters and clams along with beans and squash.

The first Canadian Thanksgiving is thought to have occurred in 1578, when an explorer, Martin Frobisher, held a Thanksgiving celebration for surviving his journey from England. Some believe that the first Thanksgiving celebrations in Canada can be traced to French settlers.

The event that Americans commonly call the "First Thanksgiving" was celebrated by the Pilgrims after their first harvest in the New World in October 1621. This feast lasted three days, and—as accounted by attendee Edward Winslow—it was attended by ninety Native Americans and fifty-three Pilgrims.

Although prayers and thanks were probably offered at the 1621 harvest gathering, the first recorded religious Thanksgiving Day in Plymouth happened two years later in 1623. On this occasion, the colonists gave thanks to God for rain after a two-month drought.

Impress your family with these Thanksgiving Day facts:

- The first Thanksgiving was held in the autumn of 1621 and included fifty Pilgrims.

- Thanksgiving didn't become a national holiday until over two hundred years later!

- There was no turkey on the menu at the first Thanksgiving, historians say. There were also no forks at the first Thanksgiving!

Why is Thanksgiving the fourth Thursday in November? President Abe Lincoln said Thanksgiving would be the fourth Thursday in November, but in 1939 President Roosevelt moved it up a week hoping it would help the shopping season during the Depression era. It never caught on, and it was changed back two years later.

The heaviest turkey on record, according to the *Guinness Book of World Records,* weighs eighty-six pounds. No forks at the first Thanksgiving! The first Thanksgiving was eaten with spoons and knives—but no forks! That's right, forks weren't even introduced to the Pilgrims until ten years later and weren't a popular utensil until the eighteenth century. Benjamin Franklin wanted the turkey to be the national bird, not the eagle.

Four Hundredth Anniversary, 2020

Material from Pilgrim Village Celebration

The four hundredth anniversary of the *Mayflower*'s landing took place in 2020. Organizations in the UK and US have planned celebrations to mark the voyage. Festivities celebrating the

anniversary have begun in various places in New England. Other celebrations are planned in England and the Netherlands, where the Pilgrims were living in exile until their voyage, but the pandemic forced some plans to be put on hold.

Among some of the events are a Mayflower Autonomous Ship, without any persons aboard, which uses an AI captain designed by IBM to self-navigate across the ocean, while the Harwich Mayflower Heritage Center is hoping to build a replica of the ship at Harwich, England. Descendants of the Pilgrims are hoping for a "once-in-alifetime" experience to commemorate their ancestors.

Girls on the Mayflower

Most of the Pilgrims felt that the bodies of girls were too weak to make the voyage on the *Mayflower* and felt that girls were not strong enough to survive the hardships of building a colony. Because of this, most parents decided to leave the girls behind in England or Holland and would send for them later once everything was built and more comfortable. Elder William Brewster brought his sons Love and Wrestling but left behind his daughters Patience and Fear. Thomas Rogers brought his son Joseph but left behind his daughters Elizabeth and Margaret. Francis Cooke brought his son John but left behind his daughters Jane and Hester. Richard Warren had five daughters—Mary, Ann, Sarah, Elizabeth, and Abigail—ranging in ages from two to ten years old, but he left them all behind. And Degory Priest also left behind his daughters Mary and Sarah.

Despite the general belief that girls were weaker, eleven girls, ranging in ages from one through seventeen, did make the voyage on the *Mayflower* with their families. And perhaps more surprisingly, young girls proved to have the strongest bodies of all: the first winter, 75 percent of the women died, 50 percent of the men died, 36 percent of the boys died, but only two girls (18 percent) died.

The youngest girl on the *Mayflower* was Humility Cooper, just about a year old. Her mother had died, so she came on the *Mayflower* in the custody of her aunt and uncle, Edward and Ann (Cooper) Tilley. Her cousin, sixteen-year-old Henry Samson, rounded out the family. Edward Tilley's brother John also brought his wife Joan, and their daughter, thirteen-year old Elizabeth Tilley. Elizabeth Tilley may have had a strong friendship with another girl, Desire Minter. Desire's father William had died in Leiden, Holland, about 1618, so she was put into the custody of John Carver, who brought her to America with him. Elizabeth would eventually name her first daughter Desire, presumably in honor of her friend.

Mayflower passenger Stephen Hopkins was the only passenger to have been to America before. Having made the voyage to Jamestown, he knew better than anyone what to expect with the voyage and in the New World. He had no problem bringing his entire family, including the girls. His eldest daughter was named Constance. She was fourteen years old. Stephen's two-year-old daughter Damaris also came. His wife, Elizabeth, was also pregnant and gave birth during the voyage to a baby boy they named Oceanus.

The Allerton family also decided to bring all their daughters. Isaac and wife, Mary Allerton, brought their daughters Remember and Mary: Remember was about six years old, and Mary was about four years old. James Chilton, the oldest passenger on the *Mayflower* at age sixty-four, brought his wife and youngest daughter, thirteen-yearold Mary Chilton, leaving his adult children behind in England and Holland.

Two other girls were on the *Mayflower* under sad circumstances. Ellen More, age eight, and Mary More, age four, were on the *Mayflower* because their father did not want them anymore; they were apparently children from his wife, Katherine, and her lover Jacob Blakeway. After "father" Samuel More discovered they were not truly his children, he and wife Katherine filed for divorce. Even though he claimed not to be the father, he won custody of the children and had them sent off to America (against their mother's wishes) with the "honest and religious" men, claiming they would have a better life outside of England where they would not suffer the social disgrace of being bastards (not born to a married couple). Perhaps it should not be surprising, then, to discover that the abandoned Ellen and Mary were the only two girls to die the first winter.

The oldest girl on the *Mayflower* was Priscilla Mullins, who was about seventeen years old. She came on the *Mayflower* with her father, William Mullins, a shoe and boot dealer, her mother Alice, and her brother Joseph. Her entire family, except for herself, died the first winter.

No girls died during the *Mayflower*'s voyage, but one boy (William Button) did. After arrival in November 1620, the girls lived on the *Mayflower* while the men went out exploring for a place to settle. The *Mayflower* sailed across to Plymouth in late December, and the men and older boys started to build the colony. The women and girls remained living on the Mayflower for much of the time while the colony was being constructed in January, February, and March.

The *Mayflower* departed back for England on April 5, after the terrible first winter was over. The first winter had left most of the girls orphaned. Elizabeth Tilley's parents John and Joan were dead, and her aunt and uncle Edward and Ann Tilley were dead as well. Mary Chilton's father and mother both died. The Allerton girls lost their mother. Desire Minter lost her adopted family of John and Katherine Carver just a couple weeks after the *Mayflower* departed. Only the Hopkins family appears to have survived the first winter unscathed.

Humility Cooper and Desire Minter both would eventually return to England after their adoptive parents died. Damaris Hopkins died sometime before 1627. All the other girls survived into adulthood, married, had families of their own, and have numerous descendants living today. Priscilla Mullins counts among her descendants such people as President John Adams, Marilyn Monroe, Vice President Dan Quayle, poets Henry Wadsworth Longfellow and William Cullem Bryant, and *War of the Worlds* director Orson Welles. Elizabeth Tilley counts among her descendants such notables as Presidents Franklin D. Roosevelt and George W. Bush, actor Humphrey Bogart, Mormon church founder Joseph Smith, and poet Ralph Waldo Emerson.

While watching television, a program on the history

channel showed two stories from 1583 on the Dare stones, entitled *Roanoke: Search for the Lost Colony*, and the second program *Return to Roanoke: Search for the Seven*.

These programs worked right into the book I have been writing for the last six months, entitled *Pilgrim's Voyage across the Ocean to a New World*, on the four hundredth anniversary Pilgrims landing in America 1620.

The Lost Colony of Roanoke

The Tale of Virginia Dare

Over thirty years before the Pilgrims landed at Plymouth Rock, a group of 117 weary men, women, and children waded ashore and made history on Roanoke Island in July 1587, establishing the first attempted settlement of its kind in the Americas.

Recruited by Sir Walter Raleigh, among these settlers was John White, his pregnant daughter, Eleanor Dare, her husband Ananias Dare, and the Indian chief Manteo, who had become an English ally during a previous visit in Britain.

They unloaded their belongings and supplies and repaired an old fort previously erected on the island. On August 18, 1587, Eleanor Dare gave birth to a daughter she named Virginia, thus earning the distinction of being the first English child born on American soil. Ten days later, John White departed for England promising to return with more supplies. It was the last time he would ever see his family.

Three years later, John White returned to Roanoke Island on his granddaughter's third birthday only to find the settlement deserted, plundered, and surrounded by overgrown brush. On one of the palisades, he found the single word "Croatoan" carved into the surface, and the letters "Cro" carved into a nearby tree. White took the carving as a sign that the colonists had moved inland to Croatoan, the home of Chief Manteo's people south of Roanoke in the Outer Banks in present-day Hatteras Island.

Before he could make further exploration, however, a great hurricane arose, damaging his ships and forcing him back to England. Despite repeated attempts, he was never able to raise the funding and resources to make the trip to America again. Raleigh had given up hope of settlement, and White died many years later on one of Raleigh's estates, ignorant of the fate of his family and the colony. The 117 pioneers of Roanoke Island had vanished into the great wilderness and into folklore. Their collective fate has been the subject of many theories and controversies, and their story is reenacted every summer during performances of *The Lost Colony*, the nation's longest symphonic drama.

Solving the Greatest Mystery in American History

Bielira, Bill, and Jim, stone mansion. Eleanor Dare stones, there were 117 columnists saluted after being ambushed. The stone Eleanor Dare cared on was a ballast stone. The ballast is for when the stones are removed from the ship's counterweight.

Lee Miller, historian: native tribes kept seven men and one woman from being saluted. The live colonists kept pounding copper. The story given to investors was a cover-up.

Father Soone After You

Goe for England Wee Cam

Hither / Onlie Misarie & Warre

Tow Yeere / Above Halfe Deade ere Tow

Yeere More From Sickenes Beine Foure & Twentie /

Salvage with Message of Shipp Unto Us / Smal

Space of Time they Affrite of Revenge Rann

Al Awaye / Wee Bleeve it Nott You / Soone After

Ye Salvages Faine Spirits Angrie / Suddaine

Murther Al Save Seaven / Mine Childe /

Ananais to Slaine wth Much Misarie /

Burie Al Neere Foure Myles Easte This River

Uppon Small Hil / Names Writ Al Ther
On Rocke / Putt This Ther Alsoe / Salvage
Shew This Unto You & Hither Wee
Promise You to Give Greate
Plentie Presents
EWD

Jamestown

Way before <u>Jamestown</u>, Roanoke Island was the first true attempt by the British to colonize the so-called New World. The mass migration got its start in 1584, when an all-male voyage, led by Sir <u>Walter Raleigh</u>, made its way into these waters. Three years later, a group of men, women, and children showed up to permanently settle the land.

The 1587 voyage to Roanoke, consisting of 118 men, women, and children, was compromised from the beginning. The failures of the previous expedition to find a suitable base from which to privateer, coupled with the lack of discovery of precious metals and other supposed treasures, led many investors to begin withdrawing support. Sir Walter Raleigh himself, even though still supportive of the idea of an English foothold in the New World, began to show a decreased enthusiasm for the venture; the colonization attempt had already cost thirty thousand pounds, a steep sum in the 1580s. Nevertheless, in April of 1587, the new group of colonists began their journey.

Led by John White, the colonists arrived at Roanoke in July, but it was not their intended destination. Roanoke Island was to only be a stopping point on this voyage so White could hopefully make contact with a very small garrison left on the island after the departure of the 1585 expedition. Instead, the colonists were to sail up the Chesapeake Bay to find a more suitable area for settlement. However, the flotilla's captain, Simon Fernandes, refused to take the colonists farther up the coast, the excuse being that summer was rapidly ending. The colonists were left at Roanoke Island.

On July 22, 1587, White and the colonists set foot on

Roanoke Island. The only clue as to the fate of the previous garrison was a sun-bleached skeleton of one of the men. The colonists got to work rebuilding and refurbishing the fortification and dwellings left by the 1585 expedition. By the end of July, they had made substantial progress. White, however, was convinced that he could move the colonists north to the Chesapeake, their intended destination, before winter.

Once again, the tenuous relationship between the English and the Algonquians broke down. Shortly after the colonists' arrival, George Howe was ambushed and killed by members of the Secotan tribe. In retaliation, White and his men attacked what they thought was a Secotan village on the mainland. It was Croatoan, stirring relationships even further.

The one bright spot in the month of August for White and the colonists was the birth of Virginia Dare, the first English child born in the New World. Her birth signified the possibility that the colony may very well take hold.

The threat of Algonquian attack, the lack of reliable food sources, and the approaching winter forced White to return to England for more settlers and supplies. White left for England in late August, having only been on Roanoke for slightly over a month. Prior to leaving, it was determined that the remaining colonists would split into two groups—one group would stay on Roanoke Island while another headed inland in search of a permanent settlement and more potential supplies. In addition, it was agreed that, should the colonists leave Roanoke Island prior to White's return, they would carve their destination into nearby trees.

John White arrived in England on November 8, 1587, and immediately reported to Sir Walter Raleigh.

The Lost Colony

In 1587, 117 English men, women, and children came ashore on Roanoke Island to establish a permanent English settlement in the New World. Just three years later in 1590, when English ships returned to bring supplies, they found the island deserted with no sign of the colonists.

The lost colony of Roanoke is one of the most notorious mysteries in American history. The cryptic clues left at the abandoned settlement and the lack of any concrete evidence make it the focus of wild speculation and theories. In the settlement's difficult founding year, its mayor, John White, left for England to request resources and manpower.

In the settlement's difficult founding year, its mayor, <u>John White</u>, left for England to request resources and manpower. He returned three years later only to find the settlement empty— his wife, child, and grandchild, <u>the first English child born in the Americas,</u> having vanished. The word Croatoan and the letters Cro, carved into trees within the colony's borders, were the only signs pointing to an explanation. Despite the clues, the returning crew was unable to search for the missing colonists. A storm approached just as they came upon the desolate settlement, forcing them to turn back for England.

On the basis of the mysterious tree carving, the nearby Croatoan Island, now known as Hatteras Island, is the location to which many believe the colonists moved. At the time of the colony's founding, the Hatteras Indians occupied the island, and a popular theory supposes that the colonists joined the group of Native Americans to overcome their lack of resources and knowledge of the land.

A supposed piece of evidence for this claim is the existence of carvings in stones that were purportedly made by Eleanor Dare, the daughter of John White. These stones, often called the Dare Stones, contain written stories that tell the fates of the colonists and personal anecdotes from Dare to her father. Though they are largely believed to be a hoax and forgery, there is some academic belief that at least one of the stones may be authentic.

Since 1998, the Croatian Project has researched and provided archaeological evidence to back up the theory that the colonists moved to be with, or at least interacted with, the Hatteras tribe. Artifacts and objects found within Croatian villages that only English settlers had owned or had made at the time have solidified the connection between the two groups. But despite this evidence, and many other theories, it is likely that no definitive answer to the mystery of the colonists' disappearance will ever be found.

The year 1587 was when the voyage to plant a second colony in Virginia Lyon commenced (120 tuns); the admiral, captained by Governor John White, with Simon Fernandez as master and pilot. A flyboat...

No plans for vessels used in the Roanoke voyages are known to exist, but reasonably accurate inferences about those vessels can be drawn from contemporary paintings, construction and performance records, woodcuts, and maritime treatises.

The wooden sailing ships of the period, while much trimmer and sleeker than their tub-like fourteenth-and fifteenth-century ancestors, had considerable strength, durability, and maneuverability. Rather than battering and slamming their way through the forces of a North Atlantic gale, the typical sixteenth-century English ship was able to slip and bob through the waves with comparative ease.

Disasters at sea were rarely caused by the structural failure of a ship. Typically, the hull or shell of the vessel was either clinker-built— that is, with plank edges overlapped and fastened with nails— or carvel-built, with planks laid flush, edge to edge, over a skeleton frame. Both methods of hull construction had advantages and drawbacks.

The clinker-built ship, while extremely strong and durable, was difficult and expensive to repair, the services of a master shipwright being required. Moreover, gun ports, which were cut through the overlapping, weakened the hull significantly. In spite of these drawbacks, the average life of a typical ship was an impressive sixtyfive years. Even though this method of construction was being phased out by the mid-1540s, it is likely that some of the vessels that took part in the Roanoke ventures were clinker-built.

The carvel-built, skeleton-frame ship was also strong, durable, and difficult to repair. The skill of a master shipwright was not always required; however, a competent carpenter could handle many repairs and alterations.

Whether a merchantman or a ship of war, a sixteenth-century vessel contained a vast array of small pieces of wood, nails, iron bolts, washers, wooden pegs, and knees or braces. All seams were made water tight with a caulking of tarred hemp fibers. The result of the shipwright's art was a springy, flexible vessel able to work under the various and variable stresses exerted by the wind; the weight of cargo, the crew, and the ship itself; and the violent impacts of the sea.

The vast majority of sixteenth-century oceangoing vessels were three-masted and square-rigged. On a square-rigged ship, the large main square sails were laced to a yard or bar, which was attached horizontally to a mast. In addition to the square sails carried on the main and foremasts, square-rigged ships of the period also had, on the aftermast, a small lateen, or triangular sail which acted as a stabilizer. The square-rigged ship of the Elizabethan era was able to sail well to windward, that is, approximately in the same direction from which the wind was blowing. The versatility of this style of rigging enabled mariners to adjust sails to meet constantly changing wind conditions. Because of the strength and durability of its hull, its maneuverability, and its adaptability, the three-masted, square-rigged ship was the mainstay of the European voyages of discovery and exploration.

In sixteenth-century England, the size of a vessel was estimated in terms of tunnage—the ship's capacity to carry 252-gallon tuns of hogshead barrels of wine. A fifty-tun ship could carry fifty hogsheads. The tun was a measure of volume, not weight, and it was hardly uniform. The capacity of a Spanish tun, for example, was considerably less than that of an English tun. Thus a Spanish vessel of fifty tuns was not the same size as a fifty-tun English ship. During the

Elizabeth Era, tonnage, a more accurate and sophisticated measurement system based on a ship's dead weight and its displacement of water, was in the early stage of development. As a system for standardizing the measurement of ship size, it was not uniformly applied to English shipping for many years thereafter. Though sometimes used interchangeably by post-Elizabethan writers, *tunnage* and *tonnage* are not synonyms.

The majority of ships used in the Roanoke ventures were privately owned, well-armed merchant ships ranging in size from twenty to four hundred tuns. Other than names and tunnage, very few details about the vessels survive. The lack of information is complicated by the inexact system for estimating ship size—one ship could be listed with different tonnages. Identification of the vessels is made more difficult—and in some cases, rendered impossible—by the Elizabethan practice of renaming ships often. Sir Francis Drake's Pelican (Golden Hind) is famous enough to be traceable, but most of the vessels associated with the Roanoke voyages are not. Contemporary descriptions of these vessels vary. A vessel called one thing in one document might be called something else in another. Further, more or less standard modern usage and definitions have little in common with sixteenth-century terminology.

Glossary of Ships

Terms from Sixteenth-Century Narratives of the
Roanoke Voyages with Contemporary Meanings

Admiral (flagship): a ship of any type on which the commander of the expedition sailed. It was usually the largest, best, or safest ship in the fleet.

Bark: a relatively small sailing vessel, generally around fifty or sixty tuns, having three masts, of which the fore and main were squarerigged, and the rearmost (mizzenmast) was rigged fore-and-aft.

Boat: a small, undecked craft propelled by oars or a small sail on a short mast. Ships' boats varied in capacity and size but always had a shallow draft. They were used to haul cargo, supplies, and personnel to and from shore. Carried aboard ships in the fleet during the Atlantic crossing, the versatile and maneuverable ship's boat played a major role in the exploration of the shallow sounds and rivers of northeastern North Carolina.

Captain: the commanding officer of a vessel, with absolute authority on board. Captains were not necessarily skilled in navigation or seamanship. Ship owners and company appointees were frequently styled captain of a ship in the fleet.

Consort: a ship of any size or type that accompanied another vessel, generally in accordance with an agreement to share any loot seized from other vessels.

Flyboat: a large ship of Dutch origin, having a high stern, broad beam, shallow draft, and one or two masts; generally squarerigged, and around six hundred tuns.

Frigate: a light, swift vessel, generally around ten tuns, having one or two square-rigged sails.

Galleass: a fighting vessel, with provisions for oar and sail power, favored by the Spanish but not by the English.

Galleon: a large, heavy, square-rigged ship, having a high stern and three or four levels or decks. The galleon design was developed primarily by Sir John Hawkins, but Spain adopted it and used it as the mainstay of its American treasure fleet.

Master: a professional mariner responsible for all aspects of sailing and maneuvering a ship.

Pilot: an experienced mariner responsible for plotting courses for ships of the fleet, particularly through coastal waters.

Pinnace: a small vessel of around twenty tuns, generally having two square-rigged masts. Pinnaces were small, fast, and maneuverable, and sometimes carried oars. They were frequently used as message boats within fleets and were also highly regarded by the English for scouting coastal waters. Some small, undecked pinnaces were technically boats, for they could be taken aboard larger vessels.

Shallop: a large, heavy undecked boat with a single fore-and-aftrigged mast.

Ship: a generic term for any square-rigged vessel having a bowsprit and three masts.

Tiltboat: a small boat with a canvas awning at the stern to provide protection from the sun.

Wherry, double wherry: an open boat used originally to carry passengers on the tidal reaches of the Thames. Noted for their great speed, wherries were sometimes called "lighthorsemen" and ranged in length from around fourteen feet for a single oarsman to twenty-fove feet for four oarsmen. The Grenville expedition of 1585 used both the tiltboat and the wherry to explore the sounds around Roanoke Island.

Ships Used in the Roanoke Voyages
1584–1590

1584: Reconnaissance voyage of Philip Amadas and Arthur Barlowe —two vessels described in Hakluyt's The Principal Navigations as "barks well furnished with men and victuals."

1585: First expedition of Sir Richard Grenville, which Planted the Lane Colony Dorothy, "a small bark" (described as a pinnace in other accounts) owned by Raleigh and possibly captioned by Barlowe.

- *Elizabeth*, a vessel of fifty tuns; Thomas Cavendish, captain.

- *Lyon (Red Lyon)* of Chichester, "a hundred tunnes or thereabouts"; George Raymond, captain.

- *Roebuck*, a flyboat of about 140 tuns; John Clarke, captain.

- *Tyger*, a ship of "seven score tun," the admiral of the fleet, commanded by Sir Richard Grenville, with Simon Fernandez, chief pilot and master. This was probably the *Tyger* originally built as a galleass in the mid-1540s and rebuilt in 1570. Its tunnage is given variously as 140, 160, and 200.

- Two pinnaces, 20 to 30 tuns each, names unknown, "for speedie seruices." One was lost on the outbound leg, so Grenville's party built its replacement at Tallaboa Bay, Puerto Rico.

- Prizes: *Santa Maria de Vincente* (300 to 400 tuns), Alonzo Cornieles, captain; a large frigate owned by Lorenzo de Vallejo; and a small frigate, used by Ralph Lane to carry salt dug at Cape Rojo, Puerto Rico.

1586: Sir Bernard Drake's voyage to Newfoundland

- *Golden Royal of Topsham* (110 tuns), owned by

Drake and Amyas Preston. Drake intended to lead Raleigh's second squadron to Virginia, but the queen ordered him to Newfoundland instead—there to seize Spaniards and warn English fishermen not to take their catches to Spain. Drake met *Lion* and maybe *Dorothy* off Newfoundland, perhaps by

- prearrangement.
- *Good Companion*, consort of *Golden Royal*.
- *Job* (70 tons), owned by Ralegh; Andrew Fulforde, captain. *Job* eventually limped into Brittany with a cargo of cedar, probably transferred from *Lion*.
- Prizes: *Lion of Viana*, a Portuguese fishing vessel; four Brazilian vessels; a French ship bound from Guinea; and seventeen other fishing vessels taken off Newfoundland.

1586: The main ships in Sir Francis Drake's fleet, which evacuated the Lane Colony

- *Aid* (200 to 250 tuns), the queen's ship; Edward Wynter, captain.
- *Bark Bond* (120 to 150 tuns), owned at least in part by John Hawkins, treasurer of the navy; Robert Crosse, captain.
- *Bark Bonner* (about 150 tuns), apparently owned by William Hawkins; George Fortescue, captain. This is the vessel that Drake offered Lane after a storm had dispersed much of the fleet.
- *Elizabeth Bonaventure* (600 tuns), the queen's ship and
- Drake's flagship.
- *Francis* (70 tuns), owned by Drake and under the command of Captain Thomas Moore. Drake offered her to Lane, but she was driven out to sea by a storm.
- *Leicester* (Ughtred), a 400-tun galleon captained by

Francis Knollys.

- *Minion of Plymouth* (100 to 200 tuns) probably owned by a consortium of Plymouth and Bristol merchants; Thomas Cely, captain; John Newsome, master.

- *Primrose* (300 tuns), partly owned by John Hawkins and captained by Martin Frobisher; its journal is an important source of information about the voyage.

- *Sea Dragon* (140 tuns), owned by Sir William Wynter, the queen's surveyor of ships; Henry Whyte, captain. Evidently one of the vessels scattered by the storm that arose while the fleet rode at anchor off the Outer Banks. In any case, on her return, she required new anchors and cables.

- *Speedwell*, a merchantman of 50 to 60 tuns; probably not the vessel of the same name that accompanied *Mayflower* in 1620. She returned to England after a storm separated her from the fleet.

- *Talbot*, a bark of 150 to 200 tuns owned by George Talbot, Earl of Shrewsbury; [Walter?] Baily, captain. This may have been one of the vessels scattered by the storm that arose while the fleet rode at anchor off the Outer Banks.

- *Thomas* (Bark Hastings, Thomas Drake, Thomas of Plymouth), a vessel of 100 to 200 tuns owned by Sir Francis Drake; Thomas Drake, captain.

- *Tyger* (200 tuns), under the command of Captain Christopher Carleill; not the Tyger of 1585.

- *White Lion* (140 to 150 tuns), a private man-of-war owned by Charles Lord Howard of Effingham. Lord Admiral of England; James Erisey, captain. She lost an anchor and cable off the Outer Banks during Drake's attempt to render assistance to the Lane colony. Eight pinnaces and a dozen or so other vessels of various kinds, including prizes.

1586: Relief voyages for the Lane Colony

- *Name unknown:* a supply ship of 100 tuns, owned and sent by Ralegh. She arrived after June 19, 1586, found Lane's settlement deserted, and soon left.
- *Names unknown:* a fleet of two large vessels and four or five smaller ones commanded by Sir Richard Greenville. Greenville arrived shortly after Ralegh's supply ship had departed. He left a holding party of fifteen men with food for two years.
- *Prizes: Brave* (Peter); *Julian of St. Brieuc* (60 tuns), Peter Godbecin, master; *Martin Johnson of Amsterdam*, a flyboat; and a bark, name unknown, taken in the Azores.

1587: The voyage to plant a second colony in Virginia

- *Lyon* (120 tuns); the admiral, captained by Governor John White, with Simon Fernandez as master and pilot. A flyboat of 20 tuns, Edward Spicer, master. A pinnace under the command of captain Edward Stafford.

1587: Sir George Carey's expedition

- *Commander* (2000 tuns), owned by Carey; William Irish, leader of the expedition, may have been her captain. Commander and two consorts left England before the squadron bearing the colonists and evidently called at Chesapeake Bay, the colonists' supposed destination, but found no evidence of English settlement. The exact relationship of Carey's expedition to White's has not been established.
- *Swallow,* a bark of 70 tuns owned by Carey.
- *Gabriel,* a pinnace of 30 tuns owned by Carey.

1588: First attempt by Governor John White to relieve the Roanoke colonists

- *Brave:* a pinnace of 30 to 50 tuns commanded by Captain Arthur Facy; Pedro Diaz, pilot.
- *Roe:* a pinnace rated at around 25 tuns.

1590: Second attempt by Governor John White to relieve the Roanoke colonists

- *Conclude*, a pinnace of 20 to 30 tuns owned by Thomas Middleton and partners; Joseph Harris, captain; Hugh Harding, master; consort of *Moonlight*.
- *Hopewell* (also known as the *Harry and John*), 140 to 160 tuns; Abraham Cocke, captain; Robert Hutton, master. Governor White booked passage on this vessel. White's account of the voyage suggests that the company barely tolerated presence even as a passenger with no real authority.
- *John Evangelist*, a pinnace, captained by William Lane.
- *Little John* (120 tuns), Christopher Newport, captain; Michael Geare, master.
- *Moonlight* (formerly Mary Terlayne), 80 tuns; owned by William Sanderson, commanded by Captain Edward Spicer.
- Two shallops lost under tow in the waters just off Plymouth.
- *Prizes: Buen Jesus of Seville* (300 to 350 tuns), *Trinidad* (60 tuns), and two Spanish frigates (one of 10 tuns).

1590: Another squadron that may have called at Roanoke Island

- *Bark Young,* owned by associates of Sir George Carey; William Irish, captain.
- *Falcon's Flight,* owned by John Norris.

(Credits: Text by Olivia Isil, edited and expanded by Lebame Houston and Wynne Dough)

Author unknown

Jamestown

Jamestown and Plymouth: Compare and Contrast

Traveling aboard the *Susan Constant*, *Godspeed,* and *Discovery,* 104 men landed in Virginia in 1607 at a place they named Jamestown. This was the first permanent English settlement in the New World.

Thirteen years later, 102 settlers aboard the *Mayflower* landed in Massachusetts at a place they named Plymouth. With these two colonies, English settlement in North America was born.

Location of the Settlements

Jamestown offered anchorage and a good defensive position. Warm climate and fertile soil allowed large plantations to prosper.

Plymouth provided good anchorage and an excellent harbor. Cold climate and thin, rocky soil limited farm size. New Englanders turned to lumbering, shipbuilding, fishing and trade.

Reasons for the Colonies

Economic motives prompted colonization in Virginia. The Virginia Company of London, organized in 1606, sponsored the Virginia Colony. Organizers of the company wanted to expand English trade and obtain a wider market for English manufactured goods. They naturally hoped for financial profit from their investment in shares of company stock.

Freedom from religious persecution motivated the Pilgrims

to leave England and settle in Holland, where there was more religious freedom. However, after a number of years, the Pilgrims felt that their children were being corrupted by the liberal Dutch lifestyle and were losing their English heritage. News of the English Colony in Virginia motivated them to leave Holland and settle in the New World.

Early Setbacks

Inexperience, unwillingness to work, and the lack of wilderness survival skills led to bickering, disagreements, and inaction at Jamestown. Poor Indian relations, disease, and the initial absence of the family unit compounded the problems.

Cooperation and hard work were part of the Pilgrim's lifestyle. Nevertheless, they, too were plagued with hunger, disease, and environmental hazards.

Religious Differences

The settlers at Jamestown were members of the Anglican faith, the official Church of England. The Pilgrims were dissenters from the Church of England and established the Puritan or Congregational Church.

Government

In 1619, the first representative legislative assembly in the New World met at the Jamestown church. It was here that our American heritage of representative government was born. Since New England was outside the jurisdiction of Virginia's government, the Pilgrims established a self-governing agreement of their own, the Mayflower Compact.

Native Americans

The Virginia colonists settled in the territory of a strong Indian empire or chiefdom. English relations with the Powhatan Indians were unstable from the beginning. Vast differences in culture, philosophies, and the English desire for dominance were obstacles too great to overcome. After the Indian uprising in 1622, the colonists gave up attempts to Christianize and live peacefully with the Powhatans.

Prior to the Pilgrims' arrival, an epidemic wiped out the majority of the New England Indians. Several survivors befriended and assisted the colonists. Good relations ended in 1636 when the Massachusetts Bay Puritans declared war on the Pequot Tribe, and Plymouth was dragged into the conflict.

Legends

Who married Pocahontas? Some erroneously believe John Smith did. In actuality, she married John Rolfe, an Englishman who started the tobacco industry in Virginia. The John Smith connection stems from Smith's later writings relating an incidence of Pocahontas saving his life.

According to Longfellow's epic, "The Courtship of Miles Standish," John Alden proposed to Priscilla Mullins on behalf of Standish, and she replied, "Why don't you speak for yourself, John?" Priscilla did, in fact, marry John Alden at Plymouth. The records do not mention Standish ever courting Priscilla.

Thanksgiving

On December 4, 1619, settlers stepped ashore at Berkeley Hundred along the James River and, in accordance with the proprietor's instruction that "the day of our ship's arrival... shall be yearly and perpetually kept as a day of thanksgiving," celebrated the first official Thanksgiving Day.

In the fall of 1621, the Pilgrims held a celebration to give thanks to God for his bounty and blessings. This occasion was the origin of the traditional Thanksgiving as we know it today.

Conclusion

The growth and development of these two English colonies, though geographically separated, contributed much to our present American heritage of law, religion, government, custom and language. As Governor Bradford of Plymouth stated:

Thus out of small beginnings greater things have been produced by His hand that made all things of nothing, and gives being to all things that are; and as one small candle may light a thousand, so the light here kindled hath shown unto many, yea, in some sort, to our whole Nation.

The charter of the Virginia Company stated:

Lastly and chiefly the way to prosper and achieve good success is to make yourselves all of one mind for the good of your country and your own, and to serve and fear God the giver of all goodness, for every plantation which our father hath not planted shall be rooted out.

Bibliography

Bradford, William. *Bradford's History*. New York: Charles Scribner's Sons, 1908.

Breen, T. H. *Puritans and Adventurers*. New York: Oxford University Press, 1980.

Hatch, Charles. *The First 17 Years*. Virginia 350th Anniversary Celebration Corporation, 1957.

Jennings, Francis. *The Invasion of America*. Chapel Hill: University of North Carolina Press, 1975.

Robbins, Roland W. *Pilgrim John Alden's Progress*. Plymouth, Massachusetts: Pilgrim Society, 1969.

Author: Nancy Fisher

Park Ranger

1985

1st Revision

John Short, Park Ranger

1994

2nd Revision

Jen Loux, William and Mary Intern

November 1995

61. Roanka Island

62. Roanka Island 2 Telvison special

See Also

- <u>Billericay</u>, where the Pilgrim fathers met prior to the voyage
- <u>Leigh-on-Sea,</u> where *Mayflower* was outfitted

- Pilgrims (Plymouth Colony)
- Puritan migration to New England (1620–1640)
- Plymouth Adventure (directed by Clarence Brown, 1952)
- *Mayflower: The Pilgrims' Adventure* (1979)
- *Mayflower II,* a replica of Mayflower in Plymouth
- Massachusetts
- *Speedwell* (1577 ship)

Notes

1. A good, strong ship was at least 300 tons, which made the *Mayflower* relatively small.

2. Cpt Jones died after coming back from a voyage to France on March 5, 1622, at about age fifty-two. For the next two years, *Mayflower* lay at her berth in Rotherhithe, not far from Jones's grave at St. Mary's Church. By 1624, she was no longer useful as a ship; her subsequent fate is unknown, but she was probably broken up about that time.

References

1. Angier, Bradford (*July 29, 2008*). *Field Guide to Medoconal Wile Plants*. Stackpole Books. <u>ISBN 9780811742801</u>, via Google Books.

2. Fraser, Rebecca. *The Mayflower, St. Martin's Press*, NY (2017).

3. Weinstein, Allen, and Rubel, David. *The Story of America*, Agincourt Press Production, (2002) pp. 60–61.

4. <u>"The Mayflower and the Birth of America"</u> Sky History.

5. *Mayflower in Plymouth Harbor" Stamp, USPS.*

6. Philbrick, Nathaniel. *Mayflower: A Story of Courage, Community, and War*, Penguin Publishing (2006) ebook ISBN:9781101218839.

7. Arber, Edward (1897). *The Story of the Pilgrim Fathers, 1606– 1623.* London: Ward and Downey. p. 286. Retrieved 19 January 2021.

8. Jackson, Kevin. *Mayflower: The Voyage from Hell,* Amazon, 2013

9. Marshall, Peter. *The Light and the Glory*, Baker Publishing Group (1977) p. 20 ISBN: 0800732715.

10. Meacham, Jon, *American Gospel: God, the Founding Fathers, and the Making of a Nation*, Random House, 2006, p. 40.

11. Hilton, Christopher. *Mayflower: The Voyage that Changed the World*, History Press (2005) ISBN:9780752495309.

12. Philbrick, Nathaniel. *Mayflower: A Story of Courage, Community, and War*, Viking (2006) ISBN:9780670037605.

13. Charles Edward Banks, p.17.

14. Whittock, Martyn. *Mayflower Lives: Pilgrims in a New World and the Early American Experience, Pegasus Books* (2019).

15. e-book ISBN: 16431332X

16. Bishop, Rev. E. W., "The Pilgrim Forefathers," *Lansing State Journal* (Michigan), Oct. 2, 1920, p. 4.

17. Arber, Edward. *The Story of the Pilgrim Fathers, 1606–1623*, Ward and Downey, Limited (1897) ISBN: 9780722266403.

18. Philbrick, Nathaniel. *Mayflower: A Story of Courage, Community and War,* (Penguin Books 2006).

19. Charles Edward Banks, *The English Ancestry and Homes of the Pilgrim Fathers Who Came to Plymouth on the* Mayflower *in 1620, the Fortune in 1621, and the Anne and* Little James *in 1623*, originally published 1929, reprint 2006 by Genealogical Publishing Co., p. 17–19.

20. Bunker, Nick. *Making Haste from Babylon: The* Mayflower *Pilgrims and their New World, a History,* Knopf, New York (2011) ISBN:0307386260.

21. Cutaway illustration of the *Mayflower*

22. Talbot, Archie Lee (1930), *A New Plymouth Colony at Kennebeck,* Brunswick: Library of Congress.

23. Lowell, James Russell (1913), *The Round Table*, Boston: Gorham Press, pp. 217–18. Next to the fugitives whom Moses led out of Egypt, the little shipload of outcasts who landed at Plymouth are destined to influence the future of the world. The spiritual thirst of mankind has for ages been quenched at Hebrew fountains; but the embodiment in human institutions of truths uttered by the Son of Man eighteen centuries ago was to be mainly the work of Puritan thought and Puritan

selfdevotion. If their municipal regulations smack somewhat of Judaism, yet there can be no nobler aim or more practical wisdom than theirs; for it was to make the law of man a living counterpart of the law of God, in their highest conception of it.

24. Ames, Azel; *William Bradford History of the Mayflower Voyage and the Destiny of Its Passenger,* Madison & Adams Press (2018), public domain (CC BY-SA 3.0) ISBN:978802 688269-5.

25. Hodgson, Godfrey. *A Great and Godly Adventure.* Public Affairs: New York, 2006.

26. Hills, Leon Clark (2009). *History and Genealogy of the Mayflower of the Planters and First Comers to Ye Olde Colonie Genealogical Publishing Com.* p. 66. ISBN:978080630775-6.

27. Barnhill, John H. (2006). "Massachusetts." In Rodney P., Carlisle; Golson, J. Geoffrey (eds.). *Colonial America from Settlement to the Revolution.* ABC-CLIO. ISBN 978-1-85109-827-9.

28. Eugene Aubrey Stratton. *Plymouth Colony: Its History and People*, 1620–1691, (Ancestry Publishing, Salt Lake City, UT,1986) p. 413.

29. Bjoern Moritz, *The Pilgrim-Fathers' Voyage with the Mayflower* (Ships on Stamps 2003)

30. Bradford, William. *History of Plymouth Plantation.* Ward and Downey, Ltd, Boston. 1896 p. 448 ISBN:9780722266410.

31. George Ernest Bowman, *The Mayflower Compact and Its Signers,* (Boston: Massachusetts Society of Mayflower Descendants, 1920). Photocopies of the 1622, 1646, and 1669 versions of the document pp. 7–19.

32. *Rich, Shebnah (1883). Truro-Cape Cod or Land Marks and Sea Marks Boston:* D. Lothrop & Co., p. 53.

33. Bradford, William. *Of Plymouth Plantation, 1620–1647,* Knopf (1952).

34. Azel Ames; William Bradford; *Bureau of Military and Civic Achievement (2018).* The Mayflower Voyage: Premium

(fourbook collection: four books in one edition detailing the history of the journey, the ship log, and the lives of its Pilgrim passengers)

35. *e-artnow.* p. <u>591</u> ISBN:9788027245062

36. Lossing, Benson John. *A Pictorial History of the United States,* Mason Bros. (1860), p. 63

37. John Harris, *Saga of the Pilgrims* (historical analysis), (Globe Newspaper Co., 1983), webpages (no links between): Uccomsaga1 and Uccom-sage.

38. Caffrey, Kate. *The Mayflower.* New York: Stein and Day, 1974.

39. Charles Edward Banks, *The English Ancestry and Homes of the Pilgrim Fathers Who Came to Plymouth on the* Mayflower *in 1620,* the Fortune *in 1621, and the* Anne *and* Little James *in 1623* (originally published: 1929 reprint: 2006 by Genealogical Publishing Co.), p. 22.

40. Charles Edward Banks, *The English Ancestry and Homes of the Pilgrim Fathers Who Came to Plymouth on* Mayflower *in 1620, the Fortune in 1621, and the* Anne *and* Little James *in 1623* (originally published: 1929, reprint: 2006 by Genealogical Publishing Co.), p. 19

41. Banks, Charles Edward. *The English Ancestry and Homes of the Pilgrim Fathers Who Came to Plymouth on the* Mayflower *in 1620, the* Fortune *in 1621, and the* Anne and Little James *in 1623* (originally published: 1929 reprint: 2006 by Genealogical Publishing Co.), p. 17.

42. "The Mayflower" *History.com.*

43. R. G. Marsden, *The Mayflower.* English Historical Review (19 October 1904), p. 677.

44. Kate Caffrey, *The Mayflower.* Rowman & Littlefield Publishers; Reissue edition (October 18, 2014), p. 324

45. Pierson, Richard E.; Pierson, Jennifer (1997). *Pierson Millennium.* Bowie, Maryland: Heritage Books, Inc. ISBN:0788407423

46. Cross-section Mayflower History

47. Johnson 2006, p.30–31

48. "The Mayflower" *History.com.*

49. Charles Edward Banks, *The English Ancestry and Homes of the Pilgrim Fathers: Who Came to Plymouth on the* Mayflower *in 1620, the* Fortune *in 1621, and the* Anne, *and the* Little James *in 1623* (Baltimore, MD.:Genealogical Publishing Co., 2006), p. 18.

50. Eugene Aubrey Stratton. *Plymouth Colony: Its History and People, 1620–1691*, (Ancestry Publishing, Salt Lake City, Utah, 1986), p. 21.

51. "William Bradford," Caleb Johnson's Mayflower History.

52. "Mayor Extends City's Freedom to the Pilgrims," *New York Tribune*, September 28, 1920.

53. *New York Herald*, November 23, 1920 p. 6.

54. "How a Great Historic Event Is to Be Celebrated throughout the Year," *The San Francisco Chronicle,* February 1, 1920 p. 2

55. "Celebrating the 400th Anniversary of the Mayflower on both sides of the Atlantic," *National Geographic*, March 15, 2020

56. "The 400th Anniversary to Remember," *The Boston Globe*, April 18, 2019, p. B2

57. The Mayflower's 400th Anniversary Celebrations Scuppered by Coronavius, *The Telegraph*, May 22, 2020.

58. "Sleek new AI Mayflower to cross Atlantic on 400th anniversary of Pilgrims' voyage" *The First News*, March 25, 2020

59. "About Us" Harwich. Mayflower Heritage Centre. Archived from the original on 14 April 2018. Retrieved 14 April 2018.

60. "2020 Commemoration by the Mayflower Society"

61. Signers of Mayflower Compact, take from each individuals' bio.

Further Reading

- Ames, Azel; Bradford, William. *History of the Mayflower Voyage and the Destiny of Its Passenger*, Madison & Adams Press (2018), public domain (CC BY-SA 3.0), ISBN: 9788026882695.

- Bradford, William (1908). Davis, William T. (ed.). *Bradford's History of Plymouth Plantation, 1606–1646*. New York: Scribners. (the only written account of the voyage).

- Marble, Annie Russel https://en.wikipedia.org/wiki/Annie_Russell_Marble (1920). *The Women Who Came in the Mayflower. Boston: Pilgrim Press.*

- Marson, R. G. (1904). "*The Mayflower.*" The English Historical

- Review. 19 (76): 669–680. JSTOR 54 8611

- Philbrick, Nathaniel (2006). *Mayflower: A Story of Courage, Community and War Viking.* ISBN 0-670-03760-5.

- Usher, Roland G (1984). *The Pilgrims and Their History.* Williamstown, Massachusetts: Corner House Publishers. ISBN 0-87928-082-4. (originally published in 1918)

- Johnson, Caleb H. (2006). *The Mayflower and Her Passengers. Indiana: Xlibris.*

- Vandrei, Martha. "The Pilgrim's Progress," *History Today* (May 2020) 70#5 pp 28–41. Covers the historiography 1629 to 2020; online.

- *Mayflower* and Plymouth History.

- Mayflower 400.

- "Woman of the Mayflower and Plymouth Colony" by Mary Soule Googins, read before the Medford Historical Society,

December 19, 1921.

- <u>Pilgrim Hall Museum</u> of Plymouth, Massachusetts.
- General Society of the Mayflower <u>Descendants</u>.
- The Mayflower and Her Log Azel Ames Project.
- <u>Project Gutenberg edition.</u>

About the Author

Walter Sawyer served in the US Navy at the age of seventeen until he was honorably discharged. Over the next twenty years, he raised his family. He enjoyed camping with his three children. Later in life, they toured most of the fifty states.

He returned to serve his country when he enlisted in the National Guard and was again called up to serve in the US Army. I received an injury while on military duty and was again honorably discharged. Now retired for thirty-five years, he enjoys the senior way of life with his seven grandchildren and five great-grandchildren.

Photo taken by Dolores E. Jewell.

www.ingramcontent.com/pod-product-compliance
Lightning Source LLC
Chambersburg PA
CBHW021654120626
46545CB00002B/860